SCOTS

in

SOUTHERN EUROPE

1600-1900

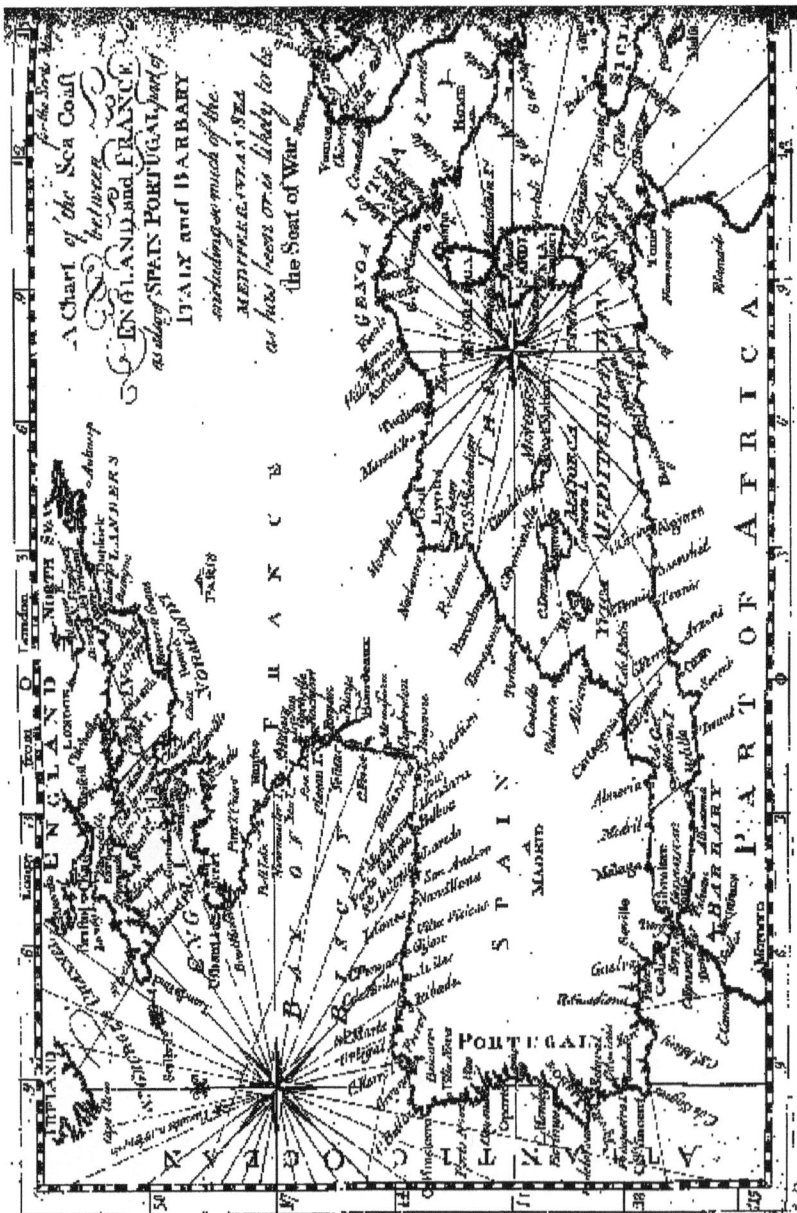

A Chart of the Sea Coast between ENGLAND and FRANCE as also of SPAIN PORTUGAL, part of ITALY and BARBARY including so much of the MEDITERRANEAN SEA as has been or is likely to be the Seat of War

ii

SCOTS
in
SOUTHERN EUROPE

1600 - 1900

*Spain, Portugal, Italy, Madeira, and
the Islands of the Mediterranean and Atlantic*

Second Edition

By
David Dobson

CLEARFIELD

Printed for Clearfield Company by
Genealogical Publishing Company
Baltimore, Maryland
2019

ISBN 9780806359021

SCOTS IN SOUTHERN EUROPE, 1600-1900: Spain, Portugal, Italy, Madeira, and the islands of the Mediterranean and Atlantic

INTRODUCTION

The countries of southern Europe attracted relatively few Scots in the early modern period. There were exceptions, of course. According to legend Scottish soldiers settled in Piedmont in the Italian Alps after the Battle of Pavia in 1525. Scots were so numerous in Rome by the late sixteenth century that a special church – Sant Andrea degli Scozzesi – was constructed for them around 1592. In any case, the vast majority of Scots found in countries such as Spain and Italy in the sixteenth and seventeenth centuries were predominantly of the Roman Catholic persuasion. For example, many sons of Scottish Catholic families were sent to colleges in Spain, Italy, or France, to complete their education, and most of them joined the priesthood.

The failure of the Jacobite Risings in 1715 and 1745 resulted in a number of Jacobites, mainly Roman Catholics and Episcopalians, taking refuge in locations within Catholic Europe, especially Italy where the Court of King James Stuart was based. Other Jacobite refugees became merchants in locations such as Madeira and Lisbon. By the eighteenth century, aristocratic families sent their sons on the Grand Tour of Europe, especially to Italy and Greece; subsequently artists and scholars settled there, some permanently others temporarily. The expansion of the British Empire during the eighteenth and nineteenth centuries led to Scottish soldiers and sailors being stationed at places such as Gibraltar and Malta, while the Iberian campaign of the Napoleonic Wars brought many Scottish fighting men to Spain and Portugal, mostly in British service but some in Portuguese service.

This volume is an expanded and revised version of an earlier work published in 2013 and contains much new data mainly derived from original research in the Regional Archives of Madeira in Funchal. Madeira was significant in transatlantic trade and emigration as many vessels made it a main port of call prior to crossing the Atlantic, or on the return journey. Possibly the first Scottish ship to do so was the Gift of God of Dundee in 1627-1628. This book contains as many as 1,800 Scots found in Spain, Portugal, Italy, Madeira, Malta, the Balearic Islands, the Azores, and the Canary Islands between 1600 and 1900.

SCOTS IN SOUTHERN EUROPE, 1600-1900

REFERENCES

AJ Aberdeen Journal

ARM Madeira Regional Archives

BRM British Residents and their problems in Madeira before
1815, [Walter Minchinton, Funchal, 1989]

CSPCol Calendar of State Papers, Colonial

DC Dundee Courier, series

DCA Dundee City Archives

DM Dundee Magazine, series

ECA Edinburgh City Archives

EMA Emigrant Ministers to America

EMG Edinburgh Medical Graduates

F   Fasti Ecclesiae Scoticanae

FPA Fulham Papers, American

GA Glasgow City Archives

GAA Amsterdam Archives

GM Gentleman's Magazine

GrA Greenock Advertiser, series

SCOTS IN SOUTHERN EUROPE, 1600-1900

G.Merc Glasgow Mercury, series

JAB Jacobites of Aberdeen and Banff, 1715, [Edinburgh 1934]

JCR Jacobite Court at Rome in 1719, [Edinburgh, 1938]

JU Jacobites at Urbino, [Basingstoke, 2009]

LC Calendar of the Laing Charters, [Edinburgh, 1899]

MAGU Matriculation Album, Glasgow University

MBR Montrose Burgess Roll

MI Monumental Inscription

NRS National Records of Scotland

OW 'Oceans of Wine', David Hancock, [Yale, 2009]

P Prisoners of the '45, [Edinburgh 1928]

PCC Prerogative Court of Canterbury

PJD People's Journal, Dundee, series

PKA Perth and Kinross Archives

RCPE Royal College of Physicians of Edinburgh

RHS Royal Historical Society

RPCS Register of Privy Council of Scotland

RSC Records of the Scots Colleges

SCOTS IN SOUTHERN EUROPE, 1600-1900

S   The Scotsman, series

SCS   Scottish Charitable Society of Boston

SG Scottish Guardian, series

SGS Scottish Genealogy Society

SHR   Scottish Historical Review

SIL   Letterbook of bailie John Steuart of Inverness, Letter-book of bailie John Steuart of Inverness, 1715-1752,[Edinburgh, 1915]

SM   Scots Magazine

SP   Scots Peerage, [Edinburgh, 1904]

TNA The National Archives of UK

W Witness, series

WKM   William Kirkpatrick of Malaga, [Grimsay Press, 2011]

SCOTS IN SOUTHERN EUROPE, 1600-1900

ABERCROMBY, JAMES FRANCIS, from the Diocese of St Andrews, a student at the Scots College in Rome, 1664. [RSC.I.117]

ABERCROMBY, JEREMY, from Edinburgh, a student at the Scots College in Rome, 1602. [RSC.I.101]

ABERCROMBY, JOHN, a student at the Scots College in Rome, 1639. [RSC.I.111]

ABERCROMBY, JOHN, at Corunna, Spain, in 1777, and in Madrid 1779, letters. [NRS.GD185.6.3.6-7]

ABERCROMBY, THOMAS CLAIR, of Glasshaugh, Banffshire, died in Rome on 3 April 1823. [Protestant Cemetery in Rome, MI]

ABERNETHY, THOMAS, a student at the Scots College in Rome, 1624, later a Jesuit. [RSC.I.107]

ADAIR, WILLIAM, late Surgeon General to the garrison in Gibraltar, died there in 1795. [SM.57.480]

ADAIR, Miss, daughter of William Adair Surgeon Major of Gibraltar, married John MacConnel of Isle Rhondo in the West Indies at Rosemount, Ayrshire, on 13 April 1793. [SM.55.256]

ADAM, ROBERT, a merchant in Malta, 1820. [NRS.CS228.A.9.2]

ADAMS, PETER, a volunteer under Garibaldi, in Italy in 1860. [SHR.57.175]

SCOTS IN SOUTHERN EUROPE, 1600-1900

ADAMSON, GEORGE, born 1671, from the Diocese of Moray, a student at the Scots College in Rome, 1690, died in Strathbogie, Aberdeenshire, on 29 May 1707. [RSC.I.122]

AIKMAN, JOHN32.208., a factor and merchant in Leghorn, [Livorno], Italy, in 1714, 1744, [NRS.AC8.172/202; AC9.1537/8]; 1721. [SIL#163]

AIKMAN, Rev. JOHN, in Funchal, Madeira, 1790, bound for Jamaica, a letter. [NRS.GD1.1429.1.10]

AIKMAN, WILLIAM, born 1682, son of William Aikman of Cairney in Angus, educated in Edinburgh University, a portrait painter, sold his estate to study in Rome in 1707, returned to Edinburgh in 1723, died in London on 7 June 1731. [misc.]

AIKMAN, WILLIAM, in Leghorn [Livorno] Italy, an entail, 8 March 1770. [NRS.RD2.208.33]

AIRE, JOHN, son of John Aire a Lieutenant of the Royal Navy, resident in Leith, an apprentice surgeon apothecary to William Ritchie in Edinburgh 1800, graduated MD from Edinburgh University in.1802, surgeon of the 31st Regiment of Foot, died in Oporto, Portugal, from fever in1809. [SM#71.878][EMG.33]

AITKEN, DAVID, an engineer in Spain, an inventory, 1876. [NRS.SC70.180/590]

AITKEN, LAUCHLAN, MD, born in Gartcows, Falkirk, on 18 March 1844, died in Rome on 19 December 1886; his wife Fanny Bouch, born in Edinburgh on 27 December 1853, eldest daughter of Sir Thomas Bouch, died in Rome on 31 May 1882. [Protestant Cemetery in Rome, MI]

SCOTS IN SOUTHERN EUROPE, 1600-1900

ALEXANDER, CATHERINE COCHRANE, born in Edinburgh on 7 February 1854, died in Rome on 10 May 1919. [Protestant Cemetery in Rome, MI]

ALEXANDER, CLAUDE, of Ballamyle, married Miss Keatinge, eldest daughter of Colonel and Lady Martha Keatinge, in the house of the British Ambassador in Florence, Italy, on 20 June 1816. [SM.78.638]

ALLAN, Mrs, wife of Thomas Allan a banker in Edinburgh, died in Turin, Italy, on 14 May 1817. [SM.79.480]

ALLEN, ELIZABETH J., born 1834, wife of James Stephen MA, a Naval instructor of the Royal Navy, later of the Turkish Navy, died in Malta on 5 July 1860. [Dalmaik MI, Aberdeenshire]

ANDERSON, ANNABELLA AGNES, born in Edinburgh on 22 January 1839, eldest daughter of Thomas Anderson, died in Rome on 3 April 1885, wife of James Anstruther. [Protestant Cemetery in Rome, MI]

ANDERSON, ARCHIBALD, from Glasgow, a student at the Scots College in Rome, 1608. [RSC.I.103]

ANDERSON, ALEXANDER, a student at the Scots College in Rome, 1642. [RSC.I.112]

ANDERSON, ALEXANDER, Lieutenant Colonel of the 12th Portuguese Infantry, late of the 42nd [Royal Highland] Regiment, married Elizabeth Bigge, eldest daughter of Thomas Bigge of Brampton Row, Middlesex, at Kensington on 2 April 1817. [SM.79.319]

ANDERSON, GEORGE, of Tulloch in Cromar, Aberdeenshire, a student at the Scots College in Madrid, Spain, 1643. [RSC.I.195]

3

SCOTS IN SOUTHERN EUROPE, 1600-1900

ANDERSON, GEORGE, an Ensign of the 26th Regiment of Foot, son of the late John Anderson a merchant in Leith, died in Portugal on 26 December 1811. [SM.74.238]

ANDERSON, or ALEXANDER, JAMES, from Aberdeen, a student at the Scots College in Rome, 1653. [RSC.I.115]

ANDERSON, JAMES, rector of the Scots College in Madrid, Spain, from 1665 to 1668. [RSC.I.202]

ANDERSON, JAMES, a Captain in Portuguese service, commander of the battalion of Lagos, died in Viana, Portugal, on 8 August 1771. [SM.33.502]

ANDERSON, JAMES, a surgeon in Oporto, Portugal, a letter, 1808. [NRS.RH1.2.777]

ANDERSON, JOHN, a student at the Scots College in Rome, 1642. [RSC.I.112]

ANDERSON, JOHN, a gentleman lately from Madeira, drowned near Staten Island, on 17 August 1763, was buried at Richmond Church. [New York Mercury, 29 August1763]

ANDERSON, JOHN, born in September 1757, son of John Anderson and his wife Henrietta Stuart in Aberdeenshire, a student at the Scots College in Rome, 1772. [RSC.I.143]

ANDERSON, JOHN, a Lieutenant of the 3rd Battalion of the Royal Scots, died at San Sebastian, Spain, on 25 June 1813. [SM.75.718]

ANDERSON, RACHEL, wife of James Wood, died 26 February 1850, buried in the British Cemetery, Funchal, Madeira. [ARM]

SCOTS IN SOUTHERN EUROPE, 1600-1900

ALEXANDER, ROBERT, from Edinburgh, a student at the Scots College in Rome, 1608. [RSC.I.102]

ANDUAGA, Don RICARDO DE GARAY Y, in Madrid, Spain, an inventory, 1879. [NRS.SC70.192/1124]

ANITUA, Don PEDRO JOSE de, sometime in Bilbao, Spain, testament, 1844, Edinburgh Sheriff Court. [NRS]

ANNAND, or WEDDERBURN, GEORGE, a student at the Scots College in Rome, 1623, later a Benedictine monk at Ratisbon, Germany. [RSC.I.107]

ANSTRUTHER, GEORGE BUCHAN, sometime a mate in the Royal Navy, died in Malta, on 2 December 1835, inventory, 1852, Commissariat of Edinburgh. [NRS]

ANTONIO, VICONT, in Madeira, 1704. [NRS.AC9.88]

APPLETON, DANIEL, a merchant in Lisbon, Portugal, an inventory, 1874. [NRS.SC70.167/575]

ARBUTHNOTT, JAMES, late Captain of HMS Avon, died in Madeira on 30 June 1817. [SM.80.98]

ARNOT, LAWRENCE, youngest son of the late Hugo Arnot of Balcorno, Fife, of the 92nd Regiment and the 12th Portuguese Regiment, died at Vittoria, Spain, on 28 July 1813. [SM.76.78]

ARTHUR, THOMAS, late of Glasgow, died in Lisbon, Portugal, during 1812. [EA#5025][SM.74.238]

ASLOAN, GEORGE, from Galloway, a student at the Scots College in Rome, 1616, later a missionary in Scotland. [RSC.I.105]

SCOTS IN SOUTHERN EUROPE, 1600-1900

ASLOAN, ROBERT, from Galloway, a student at the Scots College in Rome, 1616, died there 1617. [RSC.I.105]

AUCHENLECK, THOMAS, master of the Golden Lion of Dundee from Dundee via London to the Chesapeake in 1627, returned from Virginia via Madeira and the Baltic in 1628. [TNA.E190.31.1]

AULD, WILLIAM, in Minorca, Spain, a deed, 4 June 1779. [NRS.RD2.226/1.497]

BADENOCH, ALEXANDER, born 1776, a student at the Scots College in Valladolid, Spain, died in Edinburgh, 9 October 1836. [RSC.I.211]

BAGNALL, THOMAS, a student at the Scots College in Valladolid, Spain, 1787, a missionary as from 1794, died at New Abbey, Galloway, 27 May 1826. [RSC.I.210]

BAILLIE, ALEXANDER, a student at the Scots College in Rome, 1612, later Abbot of the Scots Monastery at Wurzburg, Germany. [RSC.I.104]

BAILLIE, GEORGE, a student at the Scots College in Rome, 1654. [RSC.I.115]

BAILLIE, JAMES, a student at the Scots College in Rome, 1625. [RSC.I.107]

BAILLIE, JAMES, a factor in Cadiz, Spain, in 1677. [NRS.AC7.4]

BAKER, ELLEN, born in Corr, Lochee, Dundee, on 13 July 1868, died in Rome on 14 August 1938. [Protestant Cemetery in Rome, MI]

SCOTS IN SOUTHERN EUROPE, 1600-1900

BALDELLI, Count, Knight of the Order of St Stephen, married Signora Lucretia Cicciaporci, only child of Signor Antonio Cicciaporci, and niece of Sir John Stuart of Allanbank, baronet, in Florence, Italy, in 1804. [SM.66.971]

BALFOUR, JAMES, a student at the Scots College in Rome, 1618. [RSC.I.106]

BALFOUR, JAMES MAITLAND, of Whittinghame, Berwickshire, died and was buried in Funchal, Madeira, 1856. [NRS.GD433.1.316; GD314.56]

BALLANTINE, ROBERT MICHAEL, a writer, born in Edinburgh on 24 April 1825, died in Rome on 8 February 1894. [Protestant Cemetery in Rome, MI]

BALLENDYNE, WILLIAM, a student at the Scots College in Rome, 1621. [RSC.I.106]

BALLENTYNE, THOMAS, from Edinburgh, a student at the Scots College in Rome, 1613. [RSC.I.104]

BALLANTINE, WILLIAM, born 1598, from Douglas, Lanarkshire, a student at the Scots College in Rome, 1641, a missionary, died in Elgin, Morayshire, 12 September 1671. [RSC.I.112]

BANNERMAN, ROBERT, from Aberdeen, a student at Padua University, Italy, in 1670. [RCPE]

BAPTISTA, JOHN, an Italian, was admitted as a burgess of Glasgow on 15 May 1633. [GBR]

BARCLAY, DAVID STUART, a Major of the 28th Regiment, died in Spain, testament, 1829, Edinburgh Sheriff Court. [NRS]

SCOTS IN SOUTHERN EUROPE, 1600-1900

BARCLAY, Reverend GEORGE, an Episcopalian chaplain, a Jacobite in Urbino, Italy, in 1717. [JU]

BARCLAY, ROBERT, born in Irvine, Ayrshire, son of Hugh Barclay and Mary Maxwell, and nephew of Father Hugh Semple, a student at the Scots College in Valladolid, Spain, 1648, at the Scots College in Rome, 1651, later a Jesuit. [RSC.I.114/198]

BARNET, HENRIETTA, born in Corfu, Greece, daughter of Henry Barnet a soldier, buried in Dundee Howff on 19 January 18-9. [DCA.burial register]

BARNS, WILLIAM, born 1845, son of Reverend Islay Barns Professor of Theology at the Free Church College in Glasgow, died 8 March 1870, buried in the British Cemetery, Funchal, Madeira. [ARM]

BARR, JOHN, a weaver in Paisley, Renfrewshire, then a soldier of the 94th Regiment of Foot, died in Spain, testament, 1813, Glasgow Sheriff Court. [NRS]

BASADRE, Don DIEGO MARIA, in Corunna, Spain, testament, 1857, Edinburgh Sheriff Court. [NRS]

BASTO, JOAO FERREIRA PINTO, Haymarket, London, died 14 August 1852, inventory 1854. Commissariat of Edinburgh. [NRS]

BAXTER, ALEXANDER, born 1810, from Edinburgh, died 22 February 1845, buried in the British Cemetery in Funchal, Madeira. [ARM]

BAUGH, MARY, second daughter of Captain Baugh of George Square, Edinburgh, married Nicolas Charles Pitt of Madeira on 10 January 1811. [SM.73.77]

SCOTS IN SOUTHERN EUROPE, 1600-1900

BAYLEY, JOHN, in Oporto, Portugal, a deed of attorney, 13 June 1775. [NRS.RD2.221/1.304]

BEATSON, ALEXANDER JOHN, of Rossend, died in Malta, 8 April 1861, inventory, 1862, Commissariat of Edinburgh. [NRS]

BEATTIE, THOMAS, born 1799, from Cruive, Dumfries-shire, died in Madeira, 21 April 1836. [ARM]

BELL, JAMES, born 1778, settled in Gibraltar in 1809, H M Inspector of Revenue and Consul for Hanover and the Netherlands, died 19 June 1866. [DA#1638]

BELL, JOHN, extra garrison surgeon, died in Gibraltar, 1799. [SM.61.724]

BELL, JOHN, born 1787, son of John Bell, [1756-1818], and his wife Ann Potter, [1755-1833], in Dumfries-shire, died in Spain on 12 August 1811. [Dornock MI,.Dumfries-shire]

BELL, JOHN, born 1762, a surgeon from Edinburgh, died 15 April 1820. [Protestant Cemetery in Rome, MI][SM.85.384]

BELL, JOHN, H.M. Consul General on Algeria, died there on 9 June 1863, inventory, 1863, Commissariat of Edinburgh. [NRS]

BELLING, JOHN, born in Milan, Italy, settled in Britain around 1794, a travelling vendor of mirrors and pictures in Scotland, 1798. [ECA.SL115.1.1]

BENNET, Major ROBERT, in Gibraltar, a deed, 30 May 1793. [NRS.RD2.258.1014]

BENNET, WILLIAM, born 1660, from the Diocese of Glasgow, a student at the Scots College in Rome, 1691. [RSC.I.122]

SCOTS IN SOUTHERN EUROPE, 1600-1900

BERRY, ANNE, second daughter of Dr Andrew Berry in Edinburgh, married Thomas Bulkley MD, in Naples, Italy, on 29 April 1826. [SM.97.766]

BETON, ALEXANDER, from Angus, a student at the Scots College in Rome, 1608. [RSC.I.102]

BETON, JAMES, a student at Padua University, Italy, in 1635. [RCPE]

BETTY, THOMAS, from Nithsdale, Dumfries-shire, a student at the Scots College in Rome, 1616, later in Paris. [RSC.I.105]

BILL, ROBERT, a student at Padua University, Italy, in 1691. [RCPE]

BISSET, JOHN, a wine merchant in Madeira around 1727. [OW.136]

BISSET and MURDOCH, merchants in Madeira trading with Gothenburg, Sweden, in 1760s. [OW.197]

BLACK, CHARLES, a secretary in Cadiz, Spain, a letter, 22 February 1719. [NRS.GD158.1710]

BLACKADDER, ARCHIBALD, in Cadiz, Spain, a deed, 1702. [NRS.RD4.91.234]

BLACKHALL, GILBERT, a student at the Scots College in Rome, 1626, later a missionary in Scotland. [RSC.I.108]

BLACKHALL, HENRY, in Naples, Italy, a deed, 29 November 1791. [NRS.RD3.255.266]

BLACKWOOD, ALEXANDER, a student at the Scots College in Rome, 1632. [RSC.I.109]

SCOTS IN SOUTHERN EUROPE, 1600-1900

BLAIR, DAVID, possibly from Kirkcudbright, in Madeira, a letter, 1833. [NRS.GD1.884.25]

BLAIR, Dr JOHN, a physician, a Jacobite in Urbino, Italy, in 1717. [JU]

BLAIR, WILLIAM RICHARDSON, born 1818, a merchant in Madeira, died and was buried in the British Cemetery, Funchal, Madeira, on 4 February, 1852. [ARM]

BLIGH, Mrs SOPHIA, wife of W. Bligh and daughter of the late Earl of Galloway, died in Madeira on 26 July 1809. [SM.71.717]

BODY, ROBERT, from Aberdeen, a student at the Scots College in Rome, 1624. RSC.I.107]

BONNER, FRANCIS, born 1777 in Berga, Tuscany, Italy, a stucco manufacturer, buried 13 June 1847 in Dundee Howff. [DCA.burial register]

BORTHWICK, HECTOR GEORGE SINCLAIR, a merchant and iron merchant in Glasgow, died in Barcelona, Spain, testament, 1864, Glasgow Sheriff Court. [NRS]

BORTHWICK, JAMES, a student at Padua University, Italy, 1669. [RCPE]

BORTHWICK, MARGARET, born 1808 in Ayrshire, died and was buried in the British Cemetery, Funchal, Madeira, on 26 January 1847. [ARM]

BORTHWICK, WILLIAM, a student at Padua University, Italy, in 1666. [RCPE]

SCOTS IN SOUTHERN EUROPE, 1600-1900

BOSWELL, THOMAS DAVID, a merchant in Valencia, Spain, son of Alexander Boswell, Lord Auchenleck, and his wife Euphemia Erskine, a genealogy, 7 May 1775. [NRS. Lyon Office][SGS]

BOURGH, GILBERT, a student at the Scots College in Rome, 1686. [RSC.I.121]

BOWERS, FRANCIS, born 1687, son of Alexander Bowers and his wife Carol Stirling in the Diocese of Brechin, a student at the Scots College in Rome, 1705. [RSC.I.126]

BOWERS, PATRICK, born 1693, son of Alexander Bowers and his wife Carol Stirling in the Diocese of Brechin, a student at the Scots College in Rome, 1709. [RSC.I.127]

BOYD, JAMES, from Angus, a student at the Scots College in Rome, 1610. [RSC.I.103]

BOYD, JOHN, from Ayrshire, then in Lisbon, Portugal, testament, 1774, Comm. Edinburgh. [NRS]

BOYD, JOHN, born 1789, of 41 Moray Place, Edinburgh, son of Thomas J Boyd, died in Madeira on 5 December 1869. [ARM]

BOYD, ROBERT, a student at Padua University, Italy, in 1626. [RCPE]

BOYD, Major General ROBERT, Lieutenant Governor of Gibraltar, was admitted as a burgess and guilds-brother of Edinburgh, on 22 July 1774. [EBR]

BOYD, Sir ROBERT, Governor of Gibraltar, Colonel of the 39th Regiment of Foot, died in Gibraltar in 1794. [SM.56.442]

SCOTS IN SOUTHERN EUROPE, 1600-1900

BOYD, THOMAS, of Caprickhill, aged 21, an Ensign of the Royal Scots, died at San Sebastian, Spain, in 1813. [SM.75.799]

BRACCI, Mrs ANN MARIA HESTER, in Italy, an inventory, 1873. [NRS.SC70.164.304]

BRACONNIER, LOUIS BARNABE, cook to J. Maitland Balfour of Whittinghame, died at Funchal, Madeira, on 11 April 1855, inventory, 1856, Commissariat of Edinburgh. [NRS]

BRANDER, JAMES, a merchant in Lisbon, Portugal, son of John Brander a merchant in Elgin, Morayshire, 1766; was granted Pitgavinie, on 3 July 1771. [NRS.RS29.VII.409; RGS.111.173]

BRANDER, MARGARET, born 1834, daughter of James Brander a wright in Dallachy and his wife Elizabeth Chrystie, died in Florence, Italy, on 26 December 1884. [Bellie MI, Morayshire]

BRANDER, WILLIAM, 'an eminent merchant in Malaga', Spain, died there in 1804. [SM.66.885]

BROCK, MARGARET MARY, wife of Alexander Robert Coldstream, MD, FRCSE, in Florence, died at the Palazzo Levi Lung, Arno Nuovo, Florence, Italy, on 27 September 1884. [S#12861]

BRODIE, JANE, daughter of the late William Brodie of Amisfield Mains, died in Siena, Italy, on 11 December 1823. [SM.93.255]

BRODIE, WILLIAM, British consul at Malaga, Spain, was admitted as a burgess of Banff in 1799. [Banff Burgess Roll]

BROOKE, NICOLAS, in Leghorn, [Livorno], Italy, a deed, 23 August 1792. [NRS.RD3.258.378]

SCOTS IN SOUTHERN EUROPE, 1600-1900

BROUGHTON, BARBARA MARY, born 1846, daughter of James Wardrop Broughton and his wife Henrietta Robina Broughton, died 22 January 1848, buried in the British Cemetery in Funchal, Madeira. [ARM]

BROUGHTON, BRIAN, born 1859, son of James Wardrop Broughton and his wife Henrietta Robina Broughton, died 29 May 1859, buried in the British Cemetery in Funchal, Madeira. [ARM]

BROUGHTON, HENRIETTA CHRISTINA, born 1845, died 19 April 1852, daughter of James Wardrop Broughton and his wife Henrietta Robina Broughton, buried in the British Cemetery in Funchal, Madeira. [ARM]

BROWN, ALEXANDER, from Aberdeen, a student at the Scots College in Rome, Italy,1638. [RSC.I.111]

BROWN, ALEXANDER, born 1829, minister of the Presbyterian Church in Madeira, died there on 19 October 1857. [Lesmahagow, Lanarkshire, MI]; buried in the British Cemetery in Funchal, Madeira. [ARM]

BROWN, FRANCES, born 30 September 1805, daughter of William Brown in Kilmarnock, Ayrshire, died in Lisbon, Portugal, on 6 April 1872, wife of Edward Medlicott. [Cemiterio dos Inglezes, Lisbon]

BROWN, GILBERT, a student at the Scots College in Rome, Italy, 1626. [RSC.I.107]

BROWN, JAMES, died in Funchal, Madeira, on 22 February 1787. [Paisley High Church MI]

SCOTS IN SOUTHERN EUROPE, 1600-1900

BROWN, JAMES LUDOVICK, born 1828, son of William Brown a merchant in Paisley, Renfrewshire, and his wife Mary Baird, died in Malaga, Spain, on 5 January 1856. [SGS]

BROWN, JOHN, son of James Brown a merchant in Edinburgh, in Madrid, Spain, 1601. [NRS.RH9.2.31]

BROWN, JOHN, in Madrid, Spain, son of James Brown a merchant burgess of Edinburgh, a letter, 1601. [NRS.RH9.2.31]

BROWN, JOHN, son of the late Thomas Brown an architect, died in Fayal, one of the Azores, on 14 June 1794. [SM.56.588]

BROWN, NEIL, HM Consul in Venice, Italy, appointed Reverend John Chalmers, a Scots minister in Veere, Zealand, as his factor in 1719. [NRS.RH11.2.1]; a merchant in Venice, 1719. [NRS.11.2.1]

BROWN, ROBERT, master of the St James, a Scots ship, before the Inquisition in the Canaries, 15 July 1591. ['The Inquisition in the Canaries', RHS, London, 1912, p.56]

BROWN, ROBERT, son of Robert Brown of Millhead and his wife Elizabeth Maxwell, a student at the Scots College in Madrid, Spain, 1721. [RSC.I.200]

BROWNE, Captain R., of the 88th Regiment of Foot, died at Pinhel, Portugal, on 25 September 1810. [SM.72.718]

BROWN, SAMUEL, born 1801, from Glasgow, died 30 November 1859, buried in the British Cemetery, Funchal, Madeira. [ARM]

BROWN, THOMAS, of Lochill, New Abbey, a student at the Scots College in Madrid, Spain, 1632. [RSC.I.195]

SCOTS IN SOUTHERN EUROPE, 1600-1900

BROWN, VALENTINE, a student at the Scots College in Rome, Italy, 1684. [RSC.I.120]

BROWN, WILLIAM, a carpenter from Leith, died in Leghorn, [Livorno], Italy, testament, 1774, Comm. Edinburgh. [NRS]

BROWN, WILLIAM, born 1846 in Peterhead, Aberdeenshire, a carpenter aboard the SS Duart Castle died and was buried in the British Cemetery, Funchal, Madeira, on 28 November 1881. [ARM]

BROWNLIE, ARCHIBALD, born 1760, British Vice Consul in Madeira, died 25 February 1834. [ARM]

BRUCE, ALEXANDER, from Aberdeen, a student at the Scots College in Rome, Italy, 1631. [RSC.I.109]

BRUCE, Captain DAVID, town adjutant of Gibraltar, 1816. [NRS.CS97.93.B5]

BRUCE, Reverend JAMES, died in Lisbon, Portugal, on 15 May 1765. [SM.27.335]

BRUCE, JOHN, from Fife, a student at the Scots College in Rome, Italy, 1613. [RSC.I.104]

BRUCE, JOHN BURNS, son of Captain David Bruce the town adjutant of Gibraltar, died 14 August 1839. [NRS.PS3.15/261]

BRUCE, MICHAEL, third son of Sir Michael Bruce of Stenhouse, baronet, died in Palermo, Sicily, on 16 July 1786. [SM.48.362]

BRUCE, Colonel, Lieutenant Colonel of the 54th Regiment of Foot, eldest son of Sir Michael Bruce of Stenhouse baronet, died in Naples, Italy, on 24 December 1791. [SM.54.49]

SCOTS IN SOUTHERN EUROPE, 1600-1900

BRUCE, ..., daughter of Gilbert Stewart Bruce, HM Consul General for the Canary Islands, was born in Teneriffe on 2 December 1818. [SM.83.190]

BRUCE, ..., daughter of A. Fairlie Bruce, was born in Paios, Huelva, Spain, on 20 May 1885. [S#13063]

BRUGH, ADAM, in Malta, a deed with Henry Fotheringham, 12 July 1807. [NRS.RD3.317.46]

BRYDEN, THOMAS, born 1805, son of Thomas Bryden and his wife Janet Valence, died in Spain during May 1837. [Biggar, Lanarkshire, MI]

BUCHAN, CHARLES, son of Thomas Buchan of Auchmacoy, died in Madeira in 2 October 1838. [AJ#4737]

BUCHAN, ..., son of Lady Buchan, was born in Lisbon, Portugal, on 23 September 1819. [SM.84.388]

BUCHANAN, GEORGE, was tried by the Inquisition in Lisbon in 1551, papers. [NLS.GB233.Adv.Ms.10.19]

BUGNI, Signor SMERALDO, teacher of Italian, Edinburgh, died 1837, inventory, 1838, Comm. Edinburgh. [NRS]

BURD, Dr WILLIAM, of the Naval Hospital, died in Gibraltar on 21 November 1804. [SM.67.76]

BURNET, ALEXANDER, from Aberdeen, a student at the Scots College in Rome, Italy, in 1667, later in Paris. [RSC.I.117]

BURNETT, ALEXANDER, son of the minister of the parish of Rayne, a student at the Scots College in Madrid, Spain, in 1699. [RSC.I.199]

SCOTS IN SOUTHERN EUROPE, 1600-1900

BURNET, DAVID, born 1638, a student at the Scots College in Rome, Italy, in 1661, died 27 December 1695. [RSC.I.117]

BURNETT, JOHN JOSEPH, from Gadsgirth, Ayr, died in Naples, Italy, on 16 March 1862. [AJ#5960]

BURNETT, THOMAS, from Edinburgh, a student at Padua University, Italy, in 1691. [RCPE]

BURNETT, WILLIAM SIMPSON, from Edinburgh, died on Madeira on 4 February 1810. [SM.72.317][ARM]

BURNS, EDWARD, a merchant in Lisbon, Portugal,1746. [NRS.AC9.1619]

BURNS, JAMES, son of Edward Burns in Lisbon, Portugal, was admitted as a merchant burgess and guilds-brother of Edinburgh, 1765. [EBR]

BURNS, WILLIAM, born 1853, son of Reverend Islay Burns, the Professor of Divinity at the Free Church College in Glasgow, died and was buried in the British Cemetery, Funchal, Madeira, on 8 March 1878. [ARM]

BUTTER, GEORGE, a student at the Scots College in Rome, Italy, 1616, died there 1617. [RSC.I.105]

CADENHEAD, or GRAY, JAMES, a student at the Scots College in Rome, Italy, in 1642. [RSC.I.112]

CADENHEAD, JAMES, a student at Padua University, Italy, in 1646. [RCPE]

CAINIE, NEIL, born 1805, from Glasgow, died in Madeira on 8 November 1827. [ARM]

SCOTS IN SOUTHERN EUROPE, 1600-1900

CALDER, ARCHIBALD, Captain of the 6th Regiment of the British Legion in Spain, an inventory, 1838, Edinburgh Sheriff Court. [NRS]

CALDER, DAVID, a General in the Service of the King of Portugal, son of Donald Calder of Straith, 1784. [NRS.CS17.1.3/52]

CALDER, JAMES, born 1781, son of James Calder a merchant in Aberdeen, [1745-1832] and his wife Anne Stephen, [1748-1829], died in Gibraltar on 7 November 1804. [St Fittick's, Nigg MI, Aberdeenshire]

CALDER, JOHN, born 1778, son of James Calder a merchant in Aberdeen, [1745-1832] and his wife Anne Stephen, [1748-1829], died in Gibraltar on 18 April 1803. [St Fittick's, Nigg MI, Aberdeenshire]

CALDERWOOD, ALEXANDER, second son of Sir William Calderwood of Dalkeith, in Padua, Italy, 1740. [Coltness Collections, 1698-1840, p.394, Glasgow 1842]

CALDWELL, JOSEPH, formerly in Milton of Grugar, now in Madeira, 1799. [NRS.CS17.1.18/116]

CALLANDER, ROBERT, a student at the Scots College in Rome, 1617, later a missionary in Scotland. [RSC.I.105]

CAMERON, ALLAN, a groom, a Jacobite in Urbino, Italy, in 1717. [JU]

CAMERON, ALEXANDER, born 8 August 1747, son of James Cameron and his wife Margery Macintosh, a student at the Scots College in Rome, 1764, in Madrid, 1795-1796, later Vicar

Apostolic in Eastern Scotland, died in Edinburgh, 8 February 1828. [NRS.NRAS.3666.38][RSC.I.140]

CAMERON, ALEXANDER, a student at the Scots College in Valladolid, Spain, 1780, Rector of the college from 1798, died 20 September 1833. [RSC.I.208]

CAMERON, ALLAN, from Lochaber, brother of Donald Cameron of Lochiel, a Jacobite in Rome by 1719. [JCR.56]

CAMPBELL, ALEXANDER, in Lima, Peru, only son of Patrick Campbell of Boath, genealogy, 17 December 1762. [NRS. Lyon Office]

CAMPBELL, Lieutenant Colonel ALLAN, Major of the 74th Regiment of Foot, and Commandant of the 3rd Regiment of Portuguese Infantry, died at Bilbao, Spain, 9 October 1813. [SM.75.960; 76.79]

CAMPBELL, ARCHIBALD, 7th Earl of Argyll, a military officer in the service of King Philip of Spain in his war against the Dutch in 1580s

CAMPBELL, ARCHIBALD, died in Minorca, Spain, in 1745. He was brother to the Earl of Hyndford and a Captain in Cotterell's Marines. [SM.7.150]

CAMPBELL, COLIN, a student at the Scots College in Rome, 1638. [RSC.I.111]

CAMPBELL, COLIN, of Ormadale, a Jacobite in Italy around 1717 later in Spain. [JCR.186]

CAMPBELL, COLIN, of Glendaruel, Argyll, a Jacobite in Rome, 1720. [JCR.192]

SCOTS IN SOUTHERN EUROPE, 1600-1900

CAMPBELL, COLIN, Lieutenant of the 55th Regiment of Foot, later Captain-Lieutenant of the 44th Regiment of Foot, died as Lieutenant Governor of Gibraltar, 1776. [SM.39.56]

CAMPBELL, COLIN, a Lieutenant General and Lieutenant Governor of Gibraltar, and commander of the forces there, died at Gibraltar on 2 April 1814. [SM]

CAMPBELL, DUGALD, Captain of the 92nd Infantry, died in Spain, 1813. [SM.76.78]

CAMPBELL, DUGALL, master of the Neptune of Glasgow, from Glasgow to Bilbao, Spain, a pass, 2 November 1706. [TNA.SP44.392.74]

CAMPBELL, DUNCAN, a Captain of the 42nd Regiment, died on 17 January 1809 from wounds received at the battle of Corunna, Spain. [SM.71.238]

CAMPBELL, HUGO, a merchant in Lisbon, Portugal, a letter, 6 April 1731. [NRS.SC14.80.3]

CAMPBELL, JAMES, a student at the Scots College in Rome, 1699. [RSC.I.124]

CAMPBELL, JANE, daughter of Colonel Alexander Campbell of Ardchattan Priory, Argyll, married Strachan J. Popham, son of the late Admiral Sir Home Popham, at the British Embassy in Florence, Italy, on 30 January 1841. [W.II.115]

CAMPBELL, JOHN, born 1711, son of Murray Campbell and his wife Joan MacLean in the Diocese of Argyll, a student at the Scots College in Rome, 1737. [RSC.I.133]

CAMPBELL Major JOHN, son of the late Dr Archibald Campbell, Professor of Church History in the University of St

SCOTS IN SOUTHERN EUROPE, 1600-1900

Andrews, died on an island near Cape Gracias a Dios on 21 August 1787. [SM.50.101]

CAMPBELL, Sir JOHN, Colonel of the 4th Portuguese Regiment of Cavalry, married Donna Maria Brigida de Faria e Lacerda, in Lisbon, Portugal, on 25 February 1816. [SM.78.398]

CAMPBELL, Captain JOHN, born 1800, from Islay, Argyll, died in Madeira on 7 August 1830. [ARM]

CAMPBELL, Brigadier General WILLIAM HOWE, in Portuguese service, a Colonel in the British Army, Lieutenant Colonel of the 31st Regiment of Foot, died in Trocifal, Portugal, on 2 January 1710. [SM.73.153]

CAMPBELL, ..., daughter of Brigadier General Sir John Campbell, was born in Lisbon, Portugal, in 1817. [SM.80.497]

CAMPBELL, LIVINGSTONE, son of Sir James Campbell of Ardinglass, Inveraray, died in Lisbon, Portugal, 7 March 1786. [Anglican Church Records, Lisbon][SM.48.155]

CAMPBELL, ROBERT, from Aberdeen, a student at the Scots College in Rome, 1687. [RSC.I.121]

CAMPBELL, Lady, wife of Sir Guy Campbell, died in Florence, Italy, on 7 May 1818. [SM.81.598]

CAMPBELL, Lieutenant General, Military Governor of Gibraltar, died there on 2 April 1814. [SM.76.399]

CARBURI, Count JOHN BAPTISTA, a noble of Cephalonia, Royal Professor of Medicine and Physician to the Royal Hospital in Turin, a member of the Academy of La Crusca, a Fellow of the Society for Botany and Natural History at Florence, was admitted as a burgess and guilds-brother of Edinburgh, on 26 June 1765. [EBR]

CARNEGIE, JAMES, born 1669, from the Diocese of St Andrews, a student at the Scots College in Rome, 1690, died in Edinburgh on 1 January 1735. [RSC.I.122]

CARNEGIE, JAMES, Earl of Southesk, born 4 April 1692 son of Charles Carnegie and his wife Mary Maitland, a Jacobite at the Battle of Sheriffmuir, fled to France in 1716, a Jacobite in Urbino, Italy, in 1717. [JAB.189] [JU]

CARNEGIE, JAMES, of Finhaven, Angus, died in Lisbon, Portugal, on 20 December 1777. [SM.40.53]

CARNEGIE, Sir JAMES, of Southesk, Angus, married Charlotte Lysons, second daughter of Rev. Daniel Lysons of Hempstead Court, Gloucestershire, in Naples, Italy, on 14 November 1825. [SM.97.126]

CARNEGIE, JOHN, of Boysack, a Jacobite in Italy after 1716, in Urbino, Italy, by 1718. [JCR.87][JU]

CARRE, THOMAS, of Cavers, died in Naples, Italy, in 1740. [SM.3.47]

CARRUTHERS, WILLIAM, in Lisbon, Portugal, died 6 May 1852, inventory, 1858, Commissariat of Edinburgh. [NRS]

CATTENACH, JOHN, a merchant in Funchal, Madeira, around 1754. [ARM][OW]

CATTENACH, WILLIAM, a student at the Scots College in Rome 1792. [RSC.I.146]

SCOTS IN SOUTHERN EUROPE, 1600-1900

CAULFIED, Mrs, daughter of the late Lord Ruthven, died in Falmouth on her return from Lisbon, Portugal, on 5 June 1785. [SM.47.312]

CAWIE, DAVID, a skipper of Dysart, Fife, master of the <u>Grace of God of Dysart,</u> at Leghorn, [Livorno], Italy, in 1629. [NRS.AC7.2/326]

CHALMERS, ALEXANDER, died 6 April 1811 on Madeira. [ARM]

CHALMER, GILBERT, from the Diocese of Aberdeen, a student at the Scots College in Rome, 1635, later a monk and Abbot of Ratisbon, Germany. [RSC.I.110]

CHALMERS, PATRICK, of Hedderwick, from Aberdeen, a student at Padua University, Italy, in 1677. [RCPE]

CHALMER, ROBERT, a student at the Scots College in Rome, in 1633. [RSC.I.110]

CHALMER, THOMAS, from Aberdeen, a student at the Scots College in Rome, in 1629. [RSC.I.109]

CHALMER, THOMAS, junior, from the Diocese of Aberdeen, a student at the Scots College in Rome, in 1630. [RSC.I.109]

CHALMER, WILLIAM, from Aberdeen, a student at the Scots College in Rome, in 1616, later a Jesuit. [RSC.I.105]

CHALMER, WILLIAM, a student at the Scots College in Rome, in 1661, later at Ratisbon, Germany. [RSC.I.117]

CHALMERS, WILLIAM, a merchant in Gibraltar, died 1755. [NLS.GB233.ms15404-15416]

24

SCOTS IN SOUTHERN EUROPE, 1600-1900

CHAMBERLAIN, PHILIP, from Edinburgh, a volunteer under Garibaldi, in Italy in 1860. [SHR.57.177]

CHAMBERS, SAMUEL, a merchant in Gibraltar, 1745. [NRS.GD1.176.5]

CHAPMAN, JAMES MILNE, MD, MRCS, from Inverness, son of Thomas Chapman, died in Madeira on 30 June 1893, aged 38. [DC#12481]

CHARETAIN, SIMONE, a merchant in Lisbon, Portugal, in 1715. [NRS.RD2.105.532]

CHARTERS, ..., son of Lieutenant Colonel Charters, was born in Lisbon, Portugal, in December 1816. [SM.78.957]

CHATTO, WILLIAM, a merchant, died in Gibraltar on 23 October 1804. [SM.67.74]

CHEAP, THOMAS, British Consul in Madeira, was admitted as a burgess and guilds-brother of Edinburgh, 27 April 1763. [EBR]; Thomas Cheap, H.M. Consul in Madeira, married Grace Stewart, daughter of the late John Stewart of Blairhall and niece of the Earl of Moray, at Inveresk on 30 June 1763, [SM.25.359]; Thomas Cheap, British Consul 1765, 1768. [TNA.CO388/95] [Cal.HOP.1766-1769.1014/1048][ARM][OW]

CHEYN, ARTHUR, from Aberdeen, a student at the Scots College in Rome, 1629. [RSC.I.109]

CHISHOLM, ANGUS, born 1759, a student at the Scots College in Valladolid, Spain, 1774, a missionary in Strathglass, Inverness-shire, Vicar Apostolic, died in Lismore, Argyll, on 28 July 1818. [RSC.I.206]

SCOTS IN SOUTHERN EUROPE, 1600-1900

CHISHOLM, ARCHIBALD, a student at the Scots College in Rome, 1616, died there in 1617. [RSC.I.105]

CHISHOLM, WILLIAM, born 1766, a student at the Scots College in Valladolid, Spain, died in Lochaber, Scotland, 30 May 1826. [RSC.I.211]

CHRISTIE, or CRICHTON, ALEXANDER, a student at the Scots College in Rome, 1674, died in Dunkirk, France, in April 1715. [RSC.I.119]

CHRISTIE, CHARLES HORACE, born 15 July 1852, eldest son of Robert Christie in Duris, Fife, died 11 April 1877. [Protestant Cemetery in Rome, MI]

CHRISTIE, JOHN, son of John Christie, a merchant, [1805-1850], and his wife Agnes Goudie, [1808-1884], died July 1870 in Pollenza, Minorca, Spain. [Cunningsburgh MI, Shetland Islands]

CHRISTIE, MARY, born 1824, daughter of C. M. Christie of Durie, Fife, wife of Francis Brown an advocate in Edinburgh, died 8 January 1848. And was buried in the British Cemetery, Funchal, Madeira. [ARM]

CIECIAPORCI, ..., daughter of the Chevalier Cieciaporci, and grand-daughter of Sir John Stuart, was born in Rome on 30 December 1785. [SM.48.50]

CICERI, JOHN, a carver and gilder in Como, Italy, died, 12 March 1865, inventory, 1865, Commissariat of Edinburgh. [NRS]

CLARK, ANDREW, Rector of the Scots College in Madrid, Spain, in 1725-1727. [RSC.I.203]

CLEGHORN, ISABELLA, born 1823, daughter of Peter Cleghorn, died in Rome during 1888. [Dunino MI, Fife]

SCOTS IN SOUTHERN EUROPE, 1600-1900

CLELAND, WILLIAM, agent for the British Linen Company, died in Madeira on 24 November 1840. [W#II/105]

CLEPHANE, Colonel WILLIAM, a Jacobite in Urbino, Italy, and later Rome from 1717. [JAB][JU]

CLERK, JAMES, born 28 January 1663, from the Diocese of Aberdeen, a student at the Scots College in Rome, 1696. [RSC.I.123]

CLERK, ROBERT, a Lieutenant of the 56th Regiment, son of George Clerk Maxwell, died in Gibraltar on 26 September 1781. [SM.43.615]

CLERK, ROBERT, son of the late Dr David Clerk a physician in Edinburgh, died in Cadiz, Spain, on 3 December 1785. [SM.47.622]

CLERK, WILLIAM, a student at Padua University, Italy, in 1665. [RCPE]

CLERK, WILLIAM, a merchant in Genoa, Italy, 1723. [GAA.NA.8599/818]

CLERK, Father WILLIAM, aged 88, confessor for about 30 years to the King of Spain, died in Madrid in 1743. He was son of William Clerk an advocate. [SM.5.428]

CLEPHAN, Colonel WILLIAM, formerly an officer in Queen Anne's Army, a Jacobite in 1715, escaped to Rome. [JCR.46]

CLINT, THOMAS, son of Thomas Clint and his wife Margharita Gregory in the Diocese of Dumfries, a student at the Scots College in Rome 1780. [RSC.I.144]

SCOTS IN SOUTHERN EUROPE, 1600-1900

CLOUGH, ARTHUR HUGH, died in Florence, Italy, on 13 November 1861, inventory, 1862, Commissariat of Edinburgh. [NRS]

COCHRAN, ALEXANDER, born on 18 August 1790, son of Reverend John Cochran and his wife Catherine Miller in Oldhamstocks, East Lothian, a merchant who died in the Canary Islands. [F.1.413]

COCK, ROBERT, aged 57, British Vice Consul in Madeira, son of William Cock a collector of Excise, died 8 April 1804. [SM.66.567]

COCKBURNE, Major JOHN, a Jacobite in Urbino, Italy, in 1717. [JU]

COLINSON, GEORGE, from Aberdeen, a student at the Scots College in Rome, 1661. [RSC.I.117]

COLLIER, Captain, a Jacobite in Urbino, Italy, 1717. [JU]

COLLISCH, GEORGE, from Dunkeld, Perthshire, son of the Baron of Balnemon, a student at the Scots College in Rome, 1626. [RSC.I.108]

COLLISON, THOMAS, a student at the Scots College in Rome, 1639. [RSC.I.111]

COLOSSI, JOSEPH, born in Venice, Italy, a dancing master in Edinburgh, 1794. [ECA.SL115.1.1]

COLQUHOUN, Sir GEORGE, of Tillquhoun, Captain of the 2nd [Queen's Royals] Regiment, was killed at Salamanca, Spain, on 23 June 1812. [SM.74.727]

SCOTS IN SOUTHERN EUROPE, 1600-1900

COLVILLE, ARCHIBALD, born 1802, from Campbeltown, Argyll, died 12 April 1858, buried in the British Cemetery in Funchal, Madeira. [ARM]

COLVILL, DAVID, from Fife, a student at the Scots College in Rome, 1608, later professor of Hebrew in the Escurial Monastery, Spain. [RSC.I.102]

CONDELL, MARTHA, 2 Broughton Place, Edinburgh, relict of Joseph Alexander Condell in Madeira, died 19 March 1829, inventory, 1828, Comm. Edinburgh. [NRS]

CONGALTON, MARY, relict of Alexander late of the Honorable East India Company Service, died in Naples, Italy, on 29 November 1849, inventory 1850, Commissariat of Edinburgh. [NRS]

CONGALTON, Mrs ROSINA AGNES, relict of John Bell a surgeon in Rome, died in Naples, Italy, on 10 September 1858, inventory, 1861, Commissariat of Edinburgh. [NRS]

CONN, FRANCIS, from Aberdeen, a student at the Scots College in Rome, 1614. [RSC.I.104]

CONN, GEORGE, from Aberdeen, a student at the Scots College in Rome, 1619. [RSC.I.106]

CONYNGHAM, JOHN, Captain of the 43rd Regiment of Foot, died in Portugal during 1796. [Anglican Church Records, Lisbon] [SM.58.650]

COOK, ELIZABETH, in Rome, an inventory, 1873. [NRS.SC70.189.667]

COOK, JOSEPH, son of Professor Cook in St Andrews, died in Madeira on 6 February 1808. [SM.70.317]

SCOTS IN SOUTHERN EUROPE, 1600-1900

COOPER, GEORGE, died in Gibraltar on 23 October 1804. [SM.67.74]

CORRIE, JOHN, born in Rome, settled in Edinburgh during 1771, a music master there in 1794. [ECA.SL115.1.1]

CORRI, NATALE, born in Rome, settled in Edinburgh in 1784, a musician with his family residing in North Hanover Street, Edinburgh in 1794. [ECA.SL115.1.1]

CORTINA, Don MANUEL DE NORIEGA, from Corunna, Spain, died 5 September 1852, inventory, Commissariat of Edinburgh. [NRS]

CORTINA, Count De La, Colonel Don Vicente Gomez de la Cortina, salcedo y Morante, Count de la Cortina, knight, died in Fuentes de Duero, Madrid, Spain, on 3 April 1842, inventory, 1844, Commissariat of Edinburgh. [NRS]

COUTTS, JAMES, a banker in London, former Member of Parliament for Edinburgh, died in Gibraltar on his return from Italy on 19 February 1778. [SM.40.111]

COUTTS, JOHN, born 28 July 1699, son of Patrick Coutts and his wife Jean Dunlop, a merchant and late Lord Provost of Edinburgh, died in Mola near Naples, Italy, on 23 March 1750. [SM.10.205]

COWPER, ..., from Aberdeen, a Captain of Artillery under Garibaldi, formerly a soldier in the Austrian army, 1860. [SHR.57.171]

CRAIGIE, THOMAS, Professor of Moral Philosophy at the University of Glasgow, died in Lisbon, Portugal, on 9 December 1751. [SM.13.597]

SCOTS IN SOUTHERN EUROPE, 1600-1900

CRANSTON, ALEXANDER, from Lauder, Peebles-shire, a student at Padua University, Italy, in 1677. [RCPE]

CRANSTOUN, GIDEON ICAEZ DE LA, of Dewar, of the firm Gordon and Company in Xeres, died in Xeres de la Frontera, Spain, on 19 November 1846; a merchant in Spain, inventory, 1847, Edinburgh Sheriff Court. [W.VII.739] [NRS]

CRAWFORD, ARCHIBALD, of Cartsburn, in Naples, Italy, a letter, 1775. [HMC.Laing.ii.470]

CRAWFORD, Lieutenant Colonel HENRY, youngest son of Archibald Crawford in Greenock, died at San Sebastian, Spain, in 1813. [SM.76.78]

CRAWFORD, PATRICK, a student at the Scots College in Rome, 1623. [RSC.I.107]

CRAWFORD, QUINTIN, from Glasgow, a student at the Scots College in Rome, 1612. [RSC.I.104]

CRAUFORD, RONALD, second son of John Crauford of Auchenames, died at Sorrento, Bay of Naples, Italy, on 18 May 1823. [SM.92.128]

CRAWFORD, WILLIAM, a merchant in Funchal, Madeira, 1620. [Tombo, Funchal Archives, codex 1503]

CRAUFORD, ..., son of John Crauford of Auchinames, was born in Florence, Italy, on 3 August 1824. [SM.94.510]

CRAWFORD, Lieutenant, of the 54th Regiment, died in Gibraltar on 30 June 1805, from wound received in a duel. [SM.67.646]

SCOTS IN SOUTHERN EUROPE, 1600-1900

CREAGH, MATTHEW, a cook, a Jacobite in Urbino, Italy, in 1717. [JU]

CREAGH, ROBERT, a secretary, a Jacobite in Urbino, Italy, in 1717. [JU]

CREIGHTON, ..., former Governor of Annamboa, Africa, died at Messina, Italy, in December 1754. [SM.16.595]

CRICHTON, HENRY, a merchant in Madeira in 1680s.

CRICHTON, JAMES, a student at the Scots College in Rome, 1642. [RSC.I.112]

CRICHTON, JOHN, and his servant, were granted a pass authorising them to travel from Falmouth to Lisbon, Portugal, on 2 November 1705. [TNA.SP44.391.155]

CRICHTON, ROBERT, from Dunkeld, Perthshire, a student at the Scots College in Rome, 1615. [RSC.I.104]

CROMAR, GEORGE, born 1796, son of Peter Cromar farmer at the Mosstoun of Cromar, Aberdeenshire, [1764-1847] and his wife Marjory McConnach, [1769-1849], a manufacturer, died 23 August 1834 in Spain. [St Peter's MI, Aberdeen]

CROSS, JOHN, a merchant from Glasgow, a factor in the Canary Islands, 1695-1703. [NRS.PC2.28.271]

CRUICKSHANK, CHARLES, born 8 January 1724, son of George Cruickshank of Robiston and his wife Anna Stuart, a student at the Scots College in Rome, 1728. Died in Edinburgh on 13 May 1788. [RSC.I.131]

SCOTS IN SOUTHERN EUROPE, 1600-1900

CUMMING, JOHN, of Naples, Italy, married Miss Magee, eldest daughter of W. Magee of the Lodge, Belfast, in Rome on 2 May 1819. [SM.84.94]

CUMMING, THOMAS, from Aberdeen, a student at the Scots College in Rome, 1602. [RSC.I.101]

CUNNINGHAM, ALEXANDER, son of Alexander Cunningham minister at Ettrick and Buccleuch, Selkirkshire, British Envoy at Venice, Italy, from 1715 to 1720. [F.2.174][NLS.GB233.ms14835/II]

CUNNINGHAM, ALEXANDER J., born in Italy around 1816, a master shoemaker in Edinburgh by 1851. [Census]

CUNNINGHAM, ALEXANDER, assistant surgeon of the 2nd Battalion, the 88th Regiment, died in Lisbon, Portugal, on 10 March 1811. [SM.73.637]

CUNNINGHAM, ARCHIBALD, in Madeira, a letter, 1827. [NRS.GD21.453]

CUNNINGHAM, CHARLES, British consul at Galatz, Turkey, died 21 November 1860, inventory 1861, Comm. Edinburgh. [NRS]

CUNNINGHAM, Sir JAMES, in Cadiz, Spain, in 1678. [NRS.AC7.4]; was admitted as a merchant and a burgess and guilds-brother of Edinburgh. [SGS][EBR]

CUNNINGHAM, JOHN, son of John Cunningham of Caddel, Ardrossan, Ayrshire, and his wife Margaret Muir, a merchant in Lisbon, Portugal, in 1739, 1754. [NRS.GD21.136/351][SGS]

SCOTS IN SOUTHERN EUROPE, 1600-1900

CUNNINGHAME, MARGARET, widow of William Thomson of Balgowan, Perthshire, died in Rome on 31 December 1904, aged 79. [Protestant Cemetery in Rome, MI]

CUNNINGHAM, Mrs MARJORY, born 1803, wife of the late General Cunningham of Newton, Perthshire, died in Rome on 9 May 1859. [Protestant Cemetery in Rome, MI]

CUNNINGHAM, PETER, from Springfield, Glasgow, a stonecutter, later a merchant seaman, a volunteer for Garibaldi in Italy in 1860. [SHR.57.169]

CUNNINGHAM, WILLIAM, son of the Baron of Drumquhassel, a student at the Scots College in Rome, 1624. [RSC.I.107]

CURRIE, WILLIAM, born 1825, son of Captain William Currie in Greenock, Renfrewshire, died 29 October 1846 in Madeira. [ARM]

CUTHBERTSON, PATRICK, a soldier in Gibraltar, dead by 1741, his widow Elizabeth Kirkwood, daughter of Alexander Kirkwood a clerk, a deed, 8 December 1741. [NRS.RD4.178/2.274]

DALRYMPLE, CHARLES, a merchant in Cadiz, Spain, was admitted as a burgess and guilds-brother of Ayr on 2 June 1757. [ABR]

DALRYMPLE, Captain ROBERT, of the 3rd Foot Guards, third son of Sir John Dalrymple of Cousland baronet, died at the Battle of Talavera de la Reyna, Spain, on 28 July 1809. [SM.71.717]

DALRYMPLE, WILLIAM, was admitted as a merchant, burgess and guilds-brother of Edinburgh in 1759; brother of Sir

SCOTS IN SOUTHERN EUROPE, 1600-1900

Hugh Dalrymple, late of Cadiz, Spain, died in Blackheath on 2 March 1782. [SM.44.165][SGS]

DALRYMPLE, ..., son of Sir Charles Dalrymple, was born in Lisbon, Portugal, in 1815. [SM.77.716]

DALYELL, ARCHIBALD, born 1740, Collector of HM Revenues and Chief Magistrate in Malta, formerly Governor in Chief of Cape Coast Castle and the British Settlements on the Gold Coast of Africa, died on Gozo, Malta, on 1 March 1818. [SM.81.499]

DALZELL, JAMES, son of Colonel John Dalzell brother of the Earl of Carnwath, a student at the Scots College in Madrid, Spain, in 1734. [RSC.I.201]

DALZELL, ROBERT ADAM, born 5 April 1792, son of Professor Andrew Dalzell and his wife Ann Drysdale in Edinburgh, British Vice Consul in Port Mahon, died in Minorca on 12 July 1860. [SGS]

DARE, Lord, son of the Earl of Selkirk, died in Florence, Italy, in 1797. [SM.59.636]

DAULING, ROBERT, a student at Padua University, Italy, in 1645. [RCPE]

D'AUSMONT, WILLIAM EUGENE GUTHRIE, MD, in Italy, an inventory, 1873. [NRS.SC70.166.471]

DAVIDSON, JOHN, from Aberdeen, a student at the Scots College in Rome, 1667. [RSC.I.117]

DAVIDSON, JOHN, a student at the Scots College in Valladolid, Spain, 1780, died in Greenock, Renfrewshire, on 8 January 1815. [RSC.I.208]

SCOTS IN SOUTHERN EUROPE, 1600-1900

DAVIDSON, JOHN GORDON, a Captain under Garibaldi, fought at the battles of Capua and Volturno, Italy, in 1860. [SHR.57.170]

DAVIDSON, ROBERT, from the Diocese of St Andrews, a student at the Scots College in Rome, 1672, died in Leith on 13 May 1711. [RSC.I.118]

DAVIDSON, ..., son of William Davidson the younger of Muirhouse, was born in Florence, Italy, on 19 August 1823. [SM.92.510]

DAWSON, ANDREW, a student at the Scots College in Valladolid, Spain, 1777, died in Huntly, Aberdeenshire, 4 September 1788. [RSC.I.207]

DAWSON, ARCHIBALD, a Scots merchant trading between London and San Miguel and Terceira in the Canaries, 1587-1588, and in Teneriffe in 1591. ['The Inquisition in the Canaries', RHS, London, 1912, p.73/74]

DAWSON, JOSEPH, son of William Dawson and his wife Anna Reid in the Diocese of Aberdeen, a student at the Scots College in Rome 1775. [RSC.I.144]

DAWSON, W., a Lieutenant of the 1st [Royal] Regiment, died at Corunna, Spain, on 15 January 1809. [SM.71.238]

DEANS, ANDREW, born 1669, from the Diocese of St Andrews, a student at the Scots College in Rome, 1694. [RSC.I.122]

DEANS, JAMES, a merchant from Edinburgh, died in Lisbon, Portugal, in 1744. [SM.6.150]

SCOTS IN SOUTHERN EUROPE, 1600-1900

DE BESCHE, JOACHIM, a merchant in Lisbon, Portugal, 1715. [NRS.RD2.105.532]

DE CASTRO, JOHN, in Madeira, 1704. [NRS.AC9.88]

DE GALLO, F., born 1828, a fencing master, possibly from Glasgow, a volunteer under Garibaldi, in Italy, 1860. [SHR.57.176]

DELLATORRE, PAUL, born in Italy, clerk to a carver and guilder in Edinburgh by 1851. [Census]

DE MONTI, C., jr., of Glasgow, died at Oporto, Portugal, on 27 January 1820. [SM.85.389]

DEMPSTER, FRANCIS, a student at the Scots College in Rome, 1628. [RSC.I.108]

DE PADUA, JEAN, a mariner aboard the St Antonio of Leghorn, [Livorno], Italy, in 1712. [NRS.AC9.428]

DICK, Sir JOHN, from Edinburgh, the British Consul in Leghorn, (Livorno), Italy, from 1767 to 1785; heir to his great-great-grandfather Sir William Dick of Braid, Edinburgh, on 14 March 1768. [NRS.GD331/42; S/H]; was admitted as a burgess and guilds-brother of Edinburgh, in 1768. [EBR]

DICKSON, DAVID, a student at Padua University, Italy, in 1666. [RCPE]

DINWIDDIE, LAURENCE, son of Gilbert Dinwiddie in Gibraltar, a deed, 3 May 1871. [NRS5/22/141]

DINWIDDIE, ROBERT, of Germiston, died in Rome on 27 April 1819. [SM.84.96]

SCOTS IN SOUTHERN EUROPE, 1600-1900

DIRKLUER, GEORGINA, born in Madeira around 1837, a servant in Edinburgh by 1851. [Census]

DI YERMO, Don ANTONIA, of Bilbao, Spain, died 21 March 1834, inventory, 1835, Comm. Edinburgh. [NRS]

DODDS, ROBERT, born 1821, from Edinburgh, died 30 May 1851, buried in the British Cemetery, Funchal, Madeira. [ARM]

DONALDSON, ANDREW, a wine merchant in Madeira in 1768. [OW.137]

DONALDSON, JAMES, bound 1660, from Aberdeen, a student at the Scots College in Rome, 1679, died in Preshome on 28 March 1740. [RSC.I.120]

D'ORFENGO, Count GEORGIO M., Captain of Artillery, Italian Army, deeds, 1886. [NRS.RD5.2057/273/21; 2065/191/83]

D'ORSEY, ALEXANDER was born in 1812, graduated MA from Glasgow University, a schoolmaster at Glasgow High School from 1834 to 1854, an Episcopalian minister in Glasgow from 1846 to 1856, then a chaplain in Madeira, died 1894. [NRS.NRAS.NA22785]

DOUGLAS, CHARLES A. W., Captain of the 51st Light Infantry, was killed in Spain, 1813. [SM.76.78]

DOUGLAS, CHARLOTTE SIDNEY, niece of William Douglas of Garvald, in Tuscany, Italy, before 1839. [SGS]

DOUGLAS, GEORGE, wrote from Burntisland, Fife, on 13 July 1698 that his next port of call would be Canary or Madeira. On 31 August he arrived at Funchal bound for Darien. [NRS.GD446.39]

SCOTS IN SOUTHERN EUROPE, 1600-1900

DOUGLAS, GEORGE, born 1681, son of Colin Douglas and his wife Elizabeth Irvine in the Diocese of Ross, a student at the Scots College in Rome, 1698, died in Morar, Inverness-shire, on 29 April 1731. [RSC.I.124]

DOUGLAS, Sir JAMES, British Consul General in Naples, Italy, married Miss Douglas sister to Alexander Douglas of Finsbury Square, London, on 22 October 1792 in Naples. [SM.54.621]

DOUGLAS, Sir JAMES, the British Consul General, died in Naples, Italy, 1795. [SM.57.411]

DOUGLAS, JESSIE CARSON, born 1826, wife of David Latta jr. in Glasgow, died 1 April 1854, and was buried in the British cemetery in Funchal, Madeira. [ARM]

DOUGLAS, ROBERT, from the Diocese of St Andrews, a student at the Scots College in Rome, 1668. [RSC.I.118]

DOUGLAS, ROBERT, in Gibraltar, brother of John Douglas a merchant in Aberdeen, a letter, 1743. [NRS.RH1.2.951]

DOUGLAS, Captain RODDAM THOMAS, of the Royal Navy, eldest son of Vice Admiral Billy Douglas, married Catherine Eliza Gourlay, eldest daughter of Dr William Gourlay of Kincraig, in Madeira on 15 July 1811. [SM.73.715]

DOUGLAS, THOMAS, a student at Padua University, Italy, in 1665. [RCPE]

DOUGLAS, WILLIAM, from Fife, a student at the Scots College in Rome, 1608. [RSC.I.102]

DOUGLAS, WILLIAM, of the family Douglas of Mordington, a student at the Scots College in Rome, 1675. [RSC.I.119]

SCOTS IN SOUTHERN EUROPE, 1600-1900

DOUGLAS, Miss, daughter of James Douglas the Consul General, married Lieutenant G. J. Harris of the Royal Navy, in Naples, Italy, in 1789. [SM.51.153]

DOVE, MARGARETTA, in Madeira, a letter, 1786. [NRS.GD21.388]

DOWNIE, Brigadier-General JOHN, Colonel of the Legion of Estremadura, Knight of the Distinguished Spanish Military Order of San Fernando, who fought for Spanish independence, was admitted as a burgess and guilds-brother of Glasgow on 19 March 1813. [GBR][see portrait, Luis Sorando Muzas, Saragoza, Spain] [TNA.WO.1.1120; 1.206]

DRUMMOND, Dr ALEXANDER MONRO, died in Naples, Italy, on 13 August 1782. [SM.44.502]

DRUMMOND, EDWARD, a student at the Scots College in Rome, 1625. [RSC.I.107]

DRUMMOND, Lord EDWARD, a Jacobite in Urbino, Italy, in 1717. [JU]

DRUMMOND, JOHN, [alias Joao Escorcio], youngest son of Sir John Drummond in Perth, settled on Madeira soon after 1425. [BRM.1] [There are letters in the NRS claiming that the Drummond family in Madeira is descended from a Lord John Drummond who settled there in the fifteenth century after having assisted Ferdinand and Isabella in the Conquest of Granada. Letters date between 1604 and 1655. [NRS]

DRUMMOND, JOHN, eldest son of the Earl of Perth, died in Lisbon, Portugal, on 13 August 1780. [SM.42.505]

SCOTS IN SOUTHERN EUROPE, 1600-1900

DRUMMOND, JOSEPH, from Strathearn, Perthshire, a student at the Scots College in Rome, 1608. [RSC.I.102]

DRUMMOND, RACHEL, daughter of James Drummond of Comrie, Perthshire, died in Oporto, Portugal, testament, 27 May 1746, Comm. Edinburgh. [NRS]

DRUMMOND, THOMAS, son of the Earl of Perth, died in Lisbon, Portugal, 13 August 1780, letters. [NRS.GD160.309]

DRUMMOND, WILLIAM, a Jacobite in Urbino, Italy, in 1717. [JU]

DRUMMMOND, Sir WILLIAM, of Logie Almond, Perthshire, born there on 9 September 1769, bound for Portugal 1789, died in Rome on 29 March 1828. [Protestant Cemetery in Rome, MI] [HMC.Laing.ii.534]

DRUMMOND, ..., Earl of Perth, a Jacobite in Urbino, Italy, in 1717. [JU]

DRYSDALE, ALEXANDER, born 21 May 1870, son of James Drysdale and his wife Euphane Young, died in Camillo, Spain, on 21 February 1897. [Tulliallan gravestone]

DUDDINGSTON, CHARLES, Captain of the 10th Regiment of Foot, died in Messina, Italy, in 1812. [SM.75.79]

DUDGEON, CHARLES, from Leith, died in Madeira, 6 January 1836. [ARM]

DUDGEON, Sir CHARLES J., born in Dumfries on 3 September 1855, formerly of Shanghai, died in San Remo, Italy, on 23 January 1928. [Protestant Cemetery in Rome, MI]

SCOTS IN SOUTHERN EUROPE, 1600-1900

DUFF, ALEXANDER, Lieutenant of the 71st Regiment of Foot, was killed in the Pyrenees in 1813. [SM.76.78]

DUFF, ALEXANDER, from Greenside, Murrayfield, late seedsman in Leith and in Edinburgh, died in Las Palmas, Grand Canary, on 27 December 1897. [S#17011]

DUFF, ANN, born in Portugal around 1845, residing in Edinburgh by 1851. [Census]. Possibly born in Lisbon on 22 April 1844. [W.V.457]

DUFF, EMILY DORA HELEN, born 1848, eldest daughter of the late Huntly George Gordon Duff of Muirtown, Inverness-shire, died of scarlet fever on 8 February 1859. [Protestant Cemetery in Rome, MI]

DUFF, HELEN, wife of Admiral Duff, and sister of the Earl of Fife, died at Gibraltar on 20 September 1778. [SM.40.567]

DUFF, JAMES, a merchant in Cadiz, Spain, was admitted as a burgess and guilds-brother of Ayr on 7 September 1781. [ABR]

DUFF, JAMES, born 1741, 'late of Madeira', died 1 April 1812. [Banff gravestone]; a wine merchant in Madeira in 1768. [OW.137]

DUFF, ROBERT, of Madeira, died in London in 1807. [SM.69.640]

DUFF, WILLIAM, born in Greenock, Renfrewshire, on 9 May 1850, died in Lisbon, Portugal, on 13 March 1914, husband of Annie Duff King. [Cemiterio dos Inglezes, Lisbon]

DUFF, ..., son of John Duff of Pitchaish, in Madeira, letters,1759-1777. [NRS.GD345.943]

SCOTS IN SOUTHERN EUROPE, 1600-1900

DUFF. ....., '"The four Duff brothers left the family farm in Strathspey to work as clerks in Edinburgh and London in the 1760s before joining their uncles James and Alexander Gordon in Madeira". [OW.140]

DUFFUS, JAMES, born 1703, son of George Duffus and his wife Anna Gordon in the Diocese of Moray, a student at the Scots College in Rome, 1721, died in Balnacraig, Scotland, 21 March 1762. [RSC.I.130]

DUNBAR, JOHN, from Edinburgh, a student at Padua University, Italy, in 1618. [RCPE]

DUNBAR, Lieutenant General THOMAS, Lieutenant Governor of Gibraltar, died in Dublin, Ireland, on 11 February 1767. [SM.29.110]

DUNBAR, WILLIAM, in Cadiz, Spain, was admitted as a burgess and guilds-brother of Ayr on 28 February 1791. [ABR]

DUNCAN, FRANK, an engineer of the P. & O. Steam Navigation Company, married Emma Gamba of Venice, Italy, there on 10 July 1884. [S#12796]

DUNCAN, HENRY, eldest son of Alexander Duncan the Clerk to the Signet, died in Madeira on 8 January 1808. [SM.70.158]

DUNCAN, JAMES, from Moray, a student at the Scots College in Rome, 1622, later in Paris. [RSC.I.106]

DUNCAN, JOHN, a merchant, died in Spain, probate 1675, PCC

DUNCANSON, Miss MARY, youngest daughter of Collector Duncanson of Campbelltown, Argyll, died in Lisbon, Portugal, on 7 March 1785. [SM.47.206]

SCOTS IN SOUTHERN EUROPE, 1600-1900

DUNDAS, Mrs AGNES, born 14 July 1852, wife of Commander C. N. Duncan, Royal Navy, of Ochtertyre, Perthshire, died 19 March 1901. [Protestant Cemetery in Rome, MI]

DUNDAS, ROBERT, son of Lord Melville, at the British Embassy in Madrid, Spain, in 1824. [NRS.GD51.10.39]

DUNDAS, ROBERT, in Madeira, in 1848. [NRS.NRAS#3246]

DUNDAS, ..., daughter of Captain D. Dundas of HMS Tagus was born in Malta in 1818. [AM.82,102]

DUNFORD, PHILIP, born in Gibraltar around 1828, residing in Edinburgh by 1851. [Census]

DURHAM, Admiral Sir PHILIP CHARLES HENDERSON CALDERWOOD, of Largo, Fife, born there on 29 July 1763, died in Naples, Italy, on 2 April 1845. [Largo MI]

DUNCAN, THOMAS, born 1799, master of the Diadem of Aberdeen died in Constantinople on March 1831. [AJ.4345]

DURNO, JAMES, 'the celebrated artist', died in Rome, August 1795. [SM.58.71]

EASSON, WILLIAM, from Edinburgh, a student at the Scots College in Rome, 1610. [RSC.I.103]

EDGAR, JAMES, a Jacobite in Urbino, Italy, in 1717; secretary to the Chevalier de St George, died in Rome, on 10 October 1762. [JU][SM.24.568]

EDMONDE, ANN EMILY, died in Rome on 3 January 1884, wife of John Smith Gairdner, born in Edinburgh, died 27 August 1889. [Protestant Cemetery in Rome, MI]

SCOTS IN SOUTHERN EUROPE, 1600-1900

EDWARD, WILLIAM, a merchant from Aberdeen, died in Funchal, Madeira, on 23 March 1841. [AJ#4870]

ELLES, MALCOLM J., a merchant in Oporto, Portugal, and Louisa Power, a marriage contract, 1842. [NRS.RD5.2072/22/137]

ELLIOT, ANDREW, youngest son of Andrew Elliot in Edinburgh, died in Madeira on 16 December 1790. [SM.53.48]

ELLIOT, JANE ANNE, born in Genoa, Italy, on 14 December 1816, daughter of George Elliot and his wife Eliza, died at Minto, Roxburghshire, on 18 January 1820. [Kelso Episcopal MI]

ELLIOT, MARIANNE, youngest daughter of Andrew Elliot of George Square, Edinburgh, died on her passage to Lisbon, Portugal, in 1789. [SM.51.155]

ELLIOT, ROBERT, born in Edinburgh, a doctor of physic, died in Bilbao, Spain, 'at a very advanced age' on 7 April 1802. [SM.64.616]

ELLIOT, WALTER, son of William Elliot and his wife Isabella Ogilvy in the diocese of St Andrews, a student at the Scots College in Rome, 1732. [RSC.I.132]

ELPHINSTONE, JAMES DALRYMPLE HORN, died on his passage to Lisbon, Portugal, on 21 April 1798. [SM.60.364]

ERSKINE, DAVID, a Writer to the Signet, died in Naples, Italy, on 5 April 1791. [SM.53.206]

ERSKINE, MARIA, widow of John Erskine, eldest son of John Erskine of Cardross, died 21 August 1824 near Rome. [Protestant Cemetery in Rome, MI][SM.94.511]

SCOTS IN SOUTHERN EUROPE, 1600-1900

ERSKINE, WILLIAM, a Jacobite in Urbino, Italy, in 1717. [JU]

ERSKINE, ..., Duke of Mar, a Jacobite in Urbino, Italy, in 1717. [JU]

"ESCORCES, GUILHERME", [William the Scot], in Funchal, Madeira, in 1599. [ARM.2]

ESDAILE, JAMES BLAIR, born 1857, son of Reverend James Esdaile and his wife Margaret Blair, died 1899 in Seville, Spain. [Rescobie gravestone, Angus]

ETTLES, ALEXANDER, aged 22, son of the late Mr Ettles in Inverness, of the House of Gordon, Shaw and Company, died in Cadiz, Spain, on 28 June 1809. [SM.71.639]

EWAN, Dr DAVID, from Ayr to Madeira in 1840, died there in 1841. [NLS.GB233.ms.15945]

EWART, WALTER, a Lieutenant of the 36th Regiment, son of John Ewart land surveyor of H.M. Customs at Greenock, Renfrewshire, died in 1812 of wounds received at the Battle of Salamanca, Spain. [SM.74.807]

FAIRRIE, JAMES, born 1821, from Greenock, Renfrewshire, died in Madeira on 21 February 1834. [SG#232][ARM]

FALCONAR, ALEXANDER ALLAN, born in Madras, India, on 27 January 1801, son of Alexander Falconar of Falcon Hall, Edinburgh, died in Rome on 8 December 1822. [Protestant Cemetery in Rome, MI]

FALCONER, GEORGE, a merchant in Cadiz, Spain, heir to his uncle Alexander Marjoribanks, a General in Dutch Service who died in December 1773, 20 June 1774. [NRS.S/H]

SCOTS IN SOUTHERN EUROPE, 1600-1900

FALCONER, ROBERT, from the Mearns, a student at the Scots College in Rome, 1613, later in Spain. [RSC.I.104]

"FANCIDE", GEORGE, a Scot in Funchal, Madeira, in 1592. [BRM.2]

FARQUHARSON, ALEXANDER, born 25 October 1758, son of Alexander Farquharson and his wife Margaret Gordon in the Diocese of Moray, a student at the Scots College in Rome 1775. [RSC.I.144]

FARQUHARSON, CHARLES, of Auchendryne, a student at the Scots College in Madrid, Spain, in 1734. [RSC.I.200]

FARQUHARSON, CHRISTINA, born in Gibraltar around 1844, with Agnes Farquharson, born in Gibraltar about 1847, residing in Edinburgh by 1851. [Census]

FARQUHARSON, FRANCES, only daughter of James Farquharson of Invercauld, died in Lisbon, Portugal, on 2 November 1788. [SM.50.571]

FARQUHARSON, JOHN, son of Gregory Farquharson and Christina Farquharson in the Diocese of Aberdeen, a student at the Scots College in Rome, 1768, died in Paris on 9 June 1811. [RSC.I.141]

FAUSSET, GEORGE, a Scots merchant trading between Barnstable, Bristol, and San Miguel in the Canaries, in 1589-1590. ['The Inquisition in the Canaries', RHS, London, 1912, p.73]

FEILD, ROBERT, born in Florence, Italy, around 1828, a letterpress journeyman in Edinburgh by 1851. [Census]

47

SCOTS IN SOUTHERN EUROPE, 1600-1900

FERGUS, JESSIE, second daughter of the late Walter Fergus of Strathore in Fife, died in Rome on 27 March 1863. [Protestant Cemetery in Rome, MI]

FERGUSON, WILLIAM, minister of the Scots Church in Limasol, Cyprus, 1878-1899. [F.7.556]

FINLAY, ANN, from Wallyford, East Lothian, died on Madeira 12 April 1810. [ARM]

FINLAY, Miss JANET, from Wallyford, East Lothian, died in Madeira on 10 November 1809. [SM.72.78][ARM]

FINLAY, WILLIAM, born 1807, from Kirkintilloch, Lanarkshire, died 6 November 1844 on board the <u>Dart of London,</u> and was buried in the British Cemetery, Funchal, Madeira. [ARM]

FINLAYSON, THOMAS, from Glasgow, died in Naples, Italy, on 22 December 1793. [SM.56.63]

FLEMING, CHARLES, a Jacobite in Urbino, Italy, in 1717. [JU]

FLEMING, ELISABETH, daughter of Dr Fleming in Glasgow. (no dates) [Protestant Cemetery in Rome, MI]

FLEMING, JAMES, aged 77, late merchant in Madeira, died in Canongate, Edinburgh, on 10 June 1814. [SM.76.639]

FLETCHER, ANDREW, agent of the Earl of Traquair in Spain, 1787-1800. [NRS.NRAS.3666.38.1.6]

FLETCHER, HARRIET, born in Portugal around 1815, residing in Edinburgh by 1851. [Census]

SCOTS IN SOUTHERN EUROPE, 1600-1900

FLETCHER, JOHN, Assistant surgeon in the Royal Navy, son of James Fletcher an Exciseman in the Canongate, died in Malta in 1809. [SM.71.878]

FONTAINE, ANGELO, born in Italy, a musician, and his wife Anna, in Edinburgh, 1794. [ECA.SL115.1.1]

FORBES, ARCHIBALD DOUGLAS, born 1881 in Aberfeldy, Perthshire, was married in the Presbyterian Church in Madeira in 1906. [ARM]

FORBES, ARTHUR, born 1631, son of James Forbes of Blackton and his wife Magdalene Fraser of Philorth, a student at the Scots College in Madrid, Spain, 1647. [RSC.I.197]

FORBES, ARTHUR, a student at the Scots College in Rome, 1650. [RSC.I.114]

FORBES, CHARLES, of Brux, a Jacobite Agent before 1715, involved in the attempt to capture Edinburgh Castle in 1715, secretary to the Old Pretender in Rome from 1718 until 1726, died in St Germains, France. [JCR.46/51]

FORBES, Sir CHARLES, of Neive and Edinglassie, died in Funchal, Madeira, on 23 May 1852. [AJ#1014]

FORBES, EDWARD JAMES DARGIE, born 1882, a banker from Dundee, died 1 May 1910, buried in the British Cemetery in Funchal, Madeira. [ARM]

FORBES, ELIZABETH COTGRAVE, daughter of John Forbes and grand-daughter of Sir Charles Forbes of Neive and Edinglassie, Aberdeenshire, died in Madeira in 17 October 1850. [AJ#5366]

SCOTS IN SOUTHERN EUROPE, 1600-1900

FORBES, JAMES, from Aberdeen, of the family of Corsenday, a student at the Scots College in Rome, 1602. [RSC.I.101]

FORBES, JOHN, born 1626, son of Duncan Forbes of Camphill in the parish of Lumphanan, Aberdeenshire, and his wife Elizabeth Forbes of Corse, a student at the Scots College in Valladolid, Spain, in 1648. [RSC.I.198]

FORBES, MARY WATSON FAENVEL, daughter of William Forbes and his wife Sarah Lawson, born 9 August 1808 and baptised in the Anglican Church of Madeira on 10 September 1808. [ARM]

FORBES, THOMAS, from Aberdeen, son of the Episcopal Bishop of Edinburgh, a student at the Scots College in Rome, in 1646. [RSC.I.113]

FORBES, WILLIAM, a student at Pisa University, Italy, in 1694. [RCPE]

FORBES, WILLIAM, a Lieutenant in the Royal Navy, youngest son of Lord Forbes, died in Lisbon, Portugal, on 1 February 1792. [SM.53.101]

FORBES, Mrs, of Callendar, Perthshire, died in Madeira on 26 March 1793. [SM.55.206]

FORBES, ..., Captain of a Regiment in Portuguese Service, married 'a young lady of a noble family there and a considerable fortune' in Lisbon, Portugal, in August 1769. [SM.31.446] Possibly Captain Forbes of Skellatur in Strathdon, Aberdeenshire, who after serving in the Prussian Army entered the service of the King of Portugal around 1763. He accompanied the Portuguese Royal Family to Brazil and died there on 8 January 1808 aged 67.

SCOTS IN SOUTHERN EUROPE, 1600-1900

FORBES, ..., daughter of Lady Forbes, was born in Messina, Sicily, on 22 August 1810. [SM.73.75]

FORESTER, ALEXANDER, born 6 August 1701, son of Alexander Forester and his spouse Christine Mackenzie of Cullenald in the Dioceses of Ross, converted to Catholicism in Paris 1726, a student at the Scots College in Rome, 1727, died in Uist, Scotland, 1780. [RSC.I.131]

FORREST, GEORGE WILLIAM, born 1787, son of John Forrest and his wife Janet Turnbull in Oaklands, Annan, Dumfries-shire, Captain of the 59th Regiment, died in Pisa, Italy, on 19 December 1818. [SGS]

FORRESTER, JOSEPH JAMES, born 1809 in Perth, to Portugal in 1831 as a merchant, created a baron by the King of Portugal in 1855. [SGS]

FORTUNE, JAMES, a bandsman of the Highland Light Infantry, died in Malta on 24 January 1898. [S#17037]

FOTHERINGHAM, JOHN, of Powrie, Angus, a Jacobite in Urbino, Italy, in 1717. [JU]

FOTHERINGHAM, ROBERT HAMILTON, born 1805, Ensign of the Bengal Infantry, only son of the late Major Fotheringham of the Madras Engineers, died in Madeira in consequence of a fall from his horse, died in Madeira on 13 June 1824. [SM.94.382][ARM]

FOUNTAIN, CHARLES, a student at the Scots College in Valladolid, Spain, 1664, died 6 October 1683. [RSC.I.198]

FRASER, ALEXANDER, from Arbroath, Angus, a volunteer under Garibaldi, in Italy, in 1860. [SHR.57.177]

SCOTS IN SOUTHERN EUROPE, 1600-1900

FRASER, ARCHIBALD CAMPBELL, former British agent and Consul General in Algiers, before 1777. [NRS.GD80.674/893]

FRASER, DUNCAN, late Judge Advocate, Commissary of Musters, and Judge of the Civil and Military Courts in Gibraltar, died on 7 November 1800. [SM.62.780]

FRASER, FRANCIS, of Findrack, born 22 August 1762, Commander in the Royal Navy and a Post Captain of the Portuguese Navy, died 24 April 1824. [Kincardine O'Neil gravestone, Aberdeenshire]

FRASER, H., born 1840, a clerk, possibly from Glasgow, a volunteer under Garibaldi, in Italy, in 1860. [SHR.57.175]

FRASER, PETER, Major of the 3rd Battalion, 1st [Royal Scots] Regiment of Foot, brother of Hugh Fraser of Eskdale, and son of Thomas Fraser of Achnacloich, died at San Sebastian in Spain on 25 June 1813. [SM.75.718]

FRASER, ..., daughter of Brigadier General H. D. Fraser, was born in Lisbon, Portugal, on 30 June 1805. [SM.67.564]

FRASER, JAMES, of Ballindown, died in Madeira during February 1791. [SM.53.203]

FRASER, JOHN, from Aberdeen, a student at the Scots College in Rome, 1608. [RSC.I.102]

FRASER, JOHN, son of John Fraser of Strathglass, Inverness-shire, and his wife Mariota Chisholm, a student at the Scots College in Madrid, 1734. [RSC.I.200]

FRASER, JOHN, born in Gibraltar around 1827, a journeyman bootmaker in Edinburgh by 1851. [Census]

SCOTS IN SOUTHERN EUROPE, 1600-1900

FRASER, or SANDEMAN, Mrs MARGARET CHISHOLM, in Rome, died 14 March 1838, inventory, 1839, Comm. Edinburgh. [NRS]

FRASER, SIMON, late a merchant in Gibraltar, 1760. [NRS.CS16.1.107/278]

FRASER, SIMON, a soldier in Portuguese service, around 1770. [NRS.GD80.893]

FRASER, SIMON, of Lovat, the younger, died in Lisbon, Portugal, in 1803. [SM.65.363]

FRASER, WILLIAM, born 1779, a student at the Scots College in Valladolid, Spain, 1794, Bishop of Arichat, Antigonish, Nova Scotia, died 4 October 1851. [RSC.I.210]

FRASER, WILLIAM WEMYSS, a Lieutenant of the 44th Regiment, youngest son of the late John Fraser in Rhives, Sutherland, died in Rome on 4 February 1826. [SM.97.511]

FRASER, ..., eldest son of Archibald Fraser of Lovat, Inverness-shire, and his wife Jane Fraser, MP and Colonel of the Fraser Fencibles, died in Lisbon, Portugal, in April 1803. [SM.78.159]

FREEBAIRN, ROBERT, a Jacobite in Urbino, Italy, in 1717. [JU]

FULLARTON, MARION BURNS, born 1828, daughter of William Fullarton, died and was buried in the British Cemetery, Funchal, Madeira, on 18 December 1852. [ARM]

FULLARTON, WILLIAM, only son of William Fullarton of Fullarton, and formerly a Lieutenant Colonel in Portuguese service, married Peggy Blair, eldest daughter of James Blair of Ardblair, at Ardblair, Perthshire, on 5 November 1765. [SM.27.558]

FULLARTON, WILLIAM, born 1802, formerly a bookseller and publisher in Glasgow, died in Funchal, Madeira, on 4 March 1844, buried in the British Cemetery, Funchal, Madeira. [ARM]; inventory, 1846, Comm. Edinburgh. [NRS] [EEC#20015][W.V.448]

FULTON, JAMES, born 1816, a merchant from Kilmarnock, Ayrshire, died in Madeira on 26 November 1847, buried in the British Cemetery in Funchal, Madeira. [ARM][EEC#21595]

FULTON, JAMES, a Professor at the Free Church Seminary in Edinburgh, died 4 April 1855, buried in the British Cemetery in Funchal, Madeira. [ARM]

FYFE, GEORGE, junior, of the Royals, eldest son of George Fyfe a coppersmith in Leith, died of wounds in Madrid, Spain, in 1812. [SM.74.807]

FYFE, THOMAS, from Aberdeen, Rector of the Scots College in Madrid, Spain, from 1715 to 1725. [RSC.I.203]

GAIRN, JAMES, son of Alexander Gairn and his wife Elizabeth Hay in the Diocese of Dunkeld, a student at the Scots College in Rome 1778. [RSC.I.144]

GARDEN, MARY ROBERTSON, born 1816, second daughter of Alexander Garden in Glasgow, died in Rome on 18 November 1834. [Protestant Cemetery in Rome, MI]

GARDINER, DAVID, from Glasgow, died in Lisbon, Portugal, in 1812. [SM.74.520]

SCOTS IN SOUTHERN EUROPE, 1600-1900

GAREOCH, ROBERT, from Aberdeen, a student at the Scots College in Rome, 1624, died there in 1625. [RSC.I.1624]

GASSIOT, JOHN PETER, formerly a Spanish merchant, later a teacher of languages in Edinburgh, 1807. [NRS.CS96.2317]

GAVIN, ANTHONY, a chaplain in Gibraltar, to Virginia in 1735, minister in St James's parish, Goochland, Va., by 1738. [EMA.29][FPA.185/187/190]

GAVIN, HUGH, born 1824, died in Malta on 29 January 1885. [S#12976]

GEBBIE, ALBERT GEORGE VALLENCE, born 1842, from Edinburgh, died 12 March 1895, buried in the British Cemetery in Funchal, Madeira. [ARM]

GEDDES, JOHN, born 29 July 1735 in the Diocese of Aberdeen, a student at the Scots College in Rome, 1750, Bishop of Morocco, 1759, Vicar Apostolic in Scotland 1769, died in Aberdeen on 11 February 1799. [RSC.I.136]

GEMMILL, KATHERINE MURDOCH DUNLOP, died in 1908. [Protestant Cemetery in Rome, MI]

GIBB, GEORGE S., born 1796 in Glasgow, died 14 March 1823 on Madeira. [ARM]

GIBB, JAMES, born 1683, son of Patrick Gibb of Fittsmyre and his wife Anna Gordon in Aberdeen, a student at the Scots College in Rome, 1704. [RSC.I.126]

GIBB, JOHN GEORGE, born 1837, son of Elias Gibb in Glasgow, died 25 July 1855, buried in the British Cemetery, Funchal, Madeira. [ARM]

SCOTS IN SOUTHERN EUROPE, 1600-1900

GIBB, JOHN, born 1840, formerly of the Edinburgh Rifle Artisan Company, a volunteer under Garibaldi, in Italy in 1860. [SHR.57.175]

GIBBON, ELIZABETH, born in Tuscany, Italy, around 1843, residing in Edinburgh, 1851. [Census]

GIBSON, D., a solicitor of taxes, died in Gibraltar on 4 November 1813; his only child James died a few days later; being the son and grandson of James Gibson a surgeon in Edinburgh. [SM.76.156]

GIBSON, WILLIAM, born in 1800, son of Robert Gibson, a flesher in Dumfries and his wife Sarah Reid, died in Portugal on 7 February 1835. [SGS]

GIFFARD, ROBERT, a student at Padua University, Italy, in 1618. [RCPE]

GILCHRIST, ELIZABETH, born in Edinburgh on 9 July 1826, died in Rome on 16 February 1905. [Protestant Cemetery in Rome, MI]

GILHAGIE, JOHN, a merchant in Glasgow, petitioned Parliament and referred to his trading voyages to the Canaries and Madeira, 1698. [APS.X.137]

GILLESPIE, OCTAVIE, born 1834, wife of Andrew Adam Gillespie of Luce, Dumfries-shire, died 28 August 1861, buried in the British Cemetery, Funchal, Madeira. [ARM]

GILLIS, JOSEPH, a wine merchant in Madeira in 1768. [OW.137]

GIUSTINELLI, GUISEPPI FRANCESCO, born in Orvietto, Italy, 'died at an advanced age after residence of nearly half a century', died at The Hirsel on 30 September 1820. The stone was placed by the Earl of Home. [Lennel MI, Berwickshire]

GLASGOW, MARY, daughter of the late John Glasgow, a merchant in Glasgow, married Charles Foote, MD, of Gibraltar, there on 19 December 1823. [SM.93.127]

GLOAG, THOMAS, a surgeon in Rome, died 26 January 1842, inventory, 1843, Commissariat of Edinburgh. [NRS]

GODSMAN, ALEXANDER, son of James Godsman and his wife
Henrietta Dunbar in the diocese of Moray, a student at the Scots College in Rome, 1732, died in Fochabers, Morayshire, Scotland, 1770. [RSC.I.132]

GODSMAN, JOHN, born June 1699, son of John Godsman and his wife Margaret Grant in the Diocese of Moray, a student at the Scots College in Rome, 1721, died in Auchinhalrig, Fochabers, Morayshire, 1 April 1769. [RSC.I.129]

GOLDIE, JAMES, born 1822 in Dumfries, son of William Goldie a bank agent, died in Madeira on 24 February 1844. [SGS]

GORDON, ADAM, a student at the Scots College in Rome, 1635, later a Jesuit missionary in Scotland. [RSC.I.110]

GORDON, ADAM LAURENCE, born 1616 in Auchmathi, Buchan, Aberdeenshire, son of George Gordon and his wife Isabell Leask, a student at the Scots College in Madrid, Spain, 1647, rector there 1655-1656. [RSC.I.196/202]

GORDON, ALEXANDER, a student at the Scots College in Rome, 1657. [RSC.I.116]

GORDON, ALEXANDER, a merchant in Madeira, 1766.

SCOTS IN SOUTHERN EUROPE, 1600-1900

[NRS.RS35.21.366; NRS.NRAS#96]

GORDON, ALEXANDER, Colonel of the 83rd Regiment, died on 28 July 1809 at the Battle of Talavera de la Reyna, Spain, aged 33. [SM.71.717]

GORDON, Lieutenant General BENJAMIN, in Bagneres de Bigorre, Spain, died 18 August 1840, inventory 1843, Commissariat of Edinburgh. [NRS]

GORDON, CARLOS PEDRO, of Wardhouse and Kildrummy, died 31 March 1876 in Madrid. [AJ.6691]

GORDON, CHARLES, born 11 September 1714, son of Adam Gordon of the Mill of Smithston and his wife Joan Gordon of Gallachys, a student at the Scots College in Rome, 1728. [RSC.I.131]

GORDON, CHARLES, a merchant in Gibraltar, deceased, father of George Alexander Gordon, and son of Alexander Gordon of Whitelay, deceased, 1784. [NRS.CS17.1.3/38]

GORDON, CHARLES, the younger of Letterfourie, son of the late Alexander Gordon of Letterfourie, died in Venice on 13 December 1805. [SM.67.238]

GORDON, CHARLES PETER, second son of John David Gordon of Wardhouse and Kildrummy, Aberdeenshire, married Ellen, youngest daughter of Joseph Prendergast, Cadiz, in Jerez de la Frontera, Spain, in January 1839. [AJ#4751]

GORDON, CHARLOTTE DOUGLAS, daughter of William Gordon in Madeira, married Archibald Inglis, from Montreal, third son of Archibald Inglis MD, FRCS Edinburgh, in New York on 27 July 1874. [S.9688]

SCOTS IN SOUTHERN EUROPE, 1600-1900

GORDON, DUFF, and Company, wine merchants in Madeira in 1807. [OW.137]

GORDON, GEORGE, born 1694, son of Alexander Gordon and his wife Anna Lumsdale in the Diocese of Moray, a student at the Scots College in Rome, 1710. [RSC.I.127]

GORDON, GEORGE, from the Diocese of Moray, a student at the Scots College in Rome, 1730. [RSC.I.132]

GORDON, GEORGE, a student at the Scots College in Valladolid, Spain, 1788, ordained 1798, a priest in Auchendown, died in Dufftown 10 May 1856. [RSC.I.210]

GORDON, J. DAVID, younger son of Wardhouse, of the house of Gordon and Company in Xerez de la Frontera, married Miss Beigbeder, only child of Peter Beigbeder a wine merchant there, in Xerez de la Frontera on 14 November 1805. [SM.67.966] James David Webster Gordon, at Quinta do Monte, Funchal, in 1780. [OW36]

GORDON, JAMES, from the Diocese of Aberdeen, a student at the Scots College in Rome, 1651, later a missionary in Scotland. [RSC.I.114]

GORDON, JAMES, born 1664, from the Diocese of Aberdeen, a student at the Scots College in Rome, 1695. [RSC.I.123]

GORDON, JAMES, a wine merchant in Madeira, trading with Europe and America, 1760-1788. [NRS.NRAS#96]

GORDON, JAMES, settled in Cadiz, third son of John Gordon of Beldorney and Margaret, daughter of Patrick Smith, third son of Patrick Smith of Braco and Methven, genealogy, 23 February 1795. [NRS.Lyon Office]

SCOTS IN SOUTHERN EUROPE, 1600-1900

GORDON, JAMES, British Consul in the Azores, 1809.
[NRS.GD51.6.1691]

GORDON, JAMES, born 1757, senior partner of the old
established house of Gordon and Company of Xerez de la
Frontera, Spain, died there on 4 October 1823. [SM.92.767]

GORDON, JAMES PETER, of Xeres de la Frontera, Spain, son
of James Gordon of Cadiz, and Rosa, daughter of Emanuel
Archinb and and Salvadora Campino of Port Royal, genealogy, 23
April 1835. [NRS.Lyon Office]

GORDON, JOHN, a student at the Scots College in Rome, 1635.
[RSC.I.110]

GORDON, JOHN, born 1672, son of James and Helen Gordon
in the Diocese of Moray, a student at the Scots College in Rome,
1697, died 11 February 1720. [RSC.I.123]

GORDON, JOHN, from the Diocese of Moray, a student at the
Scots College in Rome, 1730. [RSC.I.132]

GORDON, JOHN, born 29 May 1747, son of John Gordon and
his wife Johanna Neer in Morayshire, a student at the Scots
College in Rome 1764, rector of the Scots College in Valladoid,
1770, died at the Scots College at Valladolid, Spain, 1811.
[RSC.I.140/204]

GORDON, JOHN, a student at the Scots College in Valladolid,
Spain, 1771, died in Aberdeen. [RSC.I.205]

GORDON, JOHN, a Colonel in the service of the King of
Portugal, testament, 31 August 1785, Commissariat of Edinburgh.
[NRS]

SCOTS IN SOUTHERN EUROPE, 1600-1900

GORDON, JOHN, a student at the Scots College in Valladolid, Spain, 1774, a missionary, died in Aberdeen 1823. [RSC.I.206]

GORDON, JOHN, son of John Gordon and Mary Dawson in Tullochallum, a student at the Scots College in Rome 1792. [RSC.I.146]

GORDON, JOHN DAVID, a merchant in Jerez de la Frontera, Spain, eldest son of Charles Gordon of Wardhouse, a draft marriage contract with ......Beigbeder, daughter of Peter Beigbeder of Jerez, 1816. [NRS.GD181.85/12]

GORDON, JOHN DAVID, of Beldorney, a wine merchant residing at Xeres de la Frontera, Spain, son of Charles Gordon of Beldorney and Wardhouse, and Charlotte, daughter of Honorable Charles Boyd, son of William, 4th Earl of Kilmarnock, genealogy, 27 September 1833. [NRS. Lyon Office]

GORDON, KATHERINE ANNE CHARLOTTE, wife of Senor Don Pedro Castelli at Nizza Maritima, Spain, died before 9 May 1853. [NRS.S/H]

GORDON, or MILNE, MARGARET, Boa Vista, Oporto, Portugal, 21 April 1893. [NRS.RS.Forfar#53/146]

GORDON, PATRICK, from Aberdeen, a student at the Scots College in Rome, 1616, later at the Scots College in Paris. [RSC.I.105]

GORDON, PETER CHARLES, a wine-merchant in Spain, son of John David Gordon of Wardhouse who died on 4 August 1850. [NRS.S/H]

GORDON, ROBERT, born in Elgin, Moray, 1623, son of George Gordon and his wife Margaret Bonneyman, a student at the Scots College in Madrid, Spain, 1647. [RSC.I.197]

SCOTS IN SOUTHERN EUROPE, 1600-1900

GORDON, ROBERT, born 1669, from the Diocese of Moray, a student at the Scots College in Rome, 1694. [RSC.I.122]

GORDON, ROBERT, son of William Gordon and his wife Isabella Davidson in the Diocese of Aberdeen, a student at the Scots College in Rome, 1705. [RSC.I.126]

GORDON, ROBERT, in Portugal, a deed, 29 October 1766. [NRS.RD3.237/2.211]

GORDON, ROBERT, of Xerxes de la Frontera, Spain, married Miss Rudyard, daughter of Major Rudyard, commander of the Royal Engineers in Scotland, in 1796. [SM.58.576]

GORDON, THOMAS, a merchant in Madeira, 1782. [NRS.RS35.127]

GORDON, WILLIAM, from Aberdeen, a student at the Scots College in Rome, 1608. [RSC.I.103]

GORDON, WILLIAM, a student at Padua University, Italy, in 1621. [RCPE]

GORDON, WILLIAM, from Aberdeen, a student at the Scots College in Rome, 1669. [RSC.I.118]

GORDON, WILLIAM, son of Francis Gordon of Craig, a student at the Scots College in Madrid, 1715. [RSC.I.200]

GORDON, WILLIAM, born 1722 in the diocese of Aberdeen, a student at the Scots College in Rome, 1742. [RSC.I.134]

GORDON, Captain WILLIAM, of Kenmore, grandson and

representative of William, late Viscount of Kenmore, died in Minorca, Spain, on 7 February 1772. He was succeeded by his brother John Gordon of the 77th Regiment. [SM.34.109]

GORDON, Mrs, wife of Lieutenant Philip Gordon of the 27th Regiment of Foot, died in Gonzero, Sicily, on 29 March 1807. [SM.69.718]

GORDON, ..., wife of William Duff Gordon, died in Madrid on 1814. [SM.76.876]

GORDON, ..., son of John David Gordon the younger of Wardhouse, was born in Xerez, Spain, 1816. [SM.78.718]

GORDON, DUFF and Company, wine merchants in Madeira, 1807. [OW]

GORDON and Company, wine merchants in Madeira, trading with Europe and America, 1760-1788. [NRS.NRAS#800001]

GOURLAY, JEAN, daughter of Dr William Gourlay of Kincraig, a physician in Madeira, married Major John Austin, deputy adjutant general of the British Forces in Madeira, there on 27 September 1809. [EA.92.4783]

GOURLAY, JOHN, a student at the Scots College in Rome, 1613. [RSC.I.104]

GOURLAY, Dr WILLIAM, a physician in Madeira, married Catherine, daughter of Major Philip Van Costland of New York, in Madeira on 25 April 1787. [GM.57.637]

GOW, ROBERT LEITH, born 1858, died and was buried in the British Cemetery, Funchal, Madeira, on 13 March 1928. [ARM]

GRAEME, JOHN, a Jacobite in Urbino, Italy, in 1717. [JU]

SCOTS IN SOUTHERN EUROPE, 1600-1900

GRAEME, General, younger brother of James Graeme of Buchlyvie, a gentleman of the Duke of Montrose's family, commander in chief of the Venetian forces, died in Venice on 12 January 1767. He was formerly a Colonel in Dutch service, from which he was called by the Republic of Venice to command their forces about 12 years ago. [SM.29.55]

GRAHAM ABERNETHY, Captain of the 44th Regiment of Foot, died in Malta on 7 September 1807. [SM.69.958]

GRAHAM, ALEXANDER, British Consul in Fyal, died in 1795. [SM.57.480]

GRAHAM, HENRY, born 1809, a writer, died in Madeira on 17 April 1848, buried in the British Cemetery in Funchal, Madeira, 24 April 1848. [ARM]; son of James Graham of Ballewan, a merchant and manufacturer in Glasgow [1776-1842] and his wife Margaret Paterson [1775-1830] [Ramshorn MI, Glasgow] [ARM]

GRAHAM, JAMES, mate of the Darien Company ship the Dolphin, imprisoned in Carthagena and in Seville, Spain, in 1700, accused of piracy. [NRS. GD406.1.4541]

GRAHAM, JAMES, born 1755, youngest son of the late Robert Graham of Fintry, a Captain of the Atholl Highlanders, died in Naples on 31 January 1779. [SM.41.110]

GRAHAM, JOHN, a Colonel in the Service of the East India Company, and son of Nicol Grahame of Gartmore, died in Italy in August 1772. [SM.34.453]

GRAHAM, JOHN, a merchant in London, died in Naples on 2 October 1785. [SM.47.571]

SCOTS IN SOUTHERN EUROPE, 1600-1900

GRAHAM, NICOL, of Jarbruck, died in Malta on 1 March 1858, inventory 1858, Comm. Edinburgh. [NRS]

GRAHAM, Colonel THOMAS, of Balgowan, in Italy and Malta, 1793-1800. [NRS.GD155.1201-1291]

GRAHAM, WILLIAM, first son of Nicholas Graham of Gartmore, matriculated at Glasgow University in 1748, an advocate by 1756, died in Lisbon, Portugal, in January 1774. [MAGU][SM.37.110]

GRANT, ALEXANDER JOHN, born 1694, son of Peter Grant and his wife Anna Reid in Banff, a student at the Scots College in Rome, 1711. [RSC.I.127]

GRANT, ALEXANDER, born 1694, son of Alexander Grant and Margaret Gordon in Banff, a student at the Scots College in Rome, 1711. [RSC.I.127]

GRANT, ALEXANDER, a student at the Scots College in Valladolid, Spain, 1771, died in April 1774. [RSC.I.205]

GRANT, ALEXANDER INNES, [1843-1884], in Madeira. [NRS.GD82.480]

GRANT, JOHN MACPHERSON, son of George Grant, in Madrid, 1831-1842, Secretary to the British Legation in Portugal, 1834. [NRS.NRAS.771]

GRANT, JOHN, in Malta by 1860, son of James Grant a farmer in Tomcrocher, died 1829, and his wife Lillias Stewart, died 1840. [Abernethy, Speyside, MI]

GRANT, MARY, born in Gibraltar about 1825, a housemaid in Edinburgh in 1851. [Census]

SCOTS IN SOUTHERN EUROPE, 1600-1900

GRANT, MARY JANE, born in Madeira about 1837, residing in Edinburgh, 1851. [Census]

GRANT, PETER, Rector of the Scots College in Rome, 1745. [NRS.NRAS.3666.20.2]; Abbe Peter Grant, in Rome and Naples, letters, 1760-1765. [NRS.GD248.99.3]

GRANT, ROBERT, born 1721 in the Diocese of Moray, a student at the Scots College in Rome, 1741, died 1784 in London. [RSC.I.134]

GRANT, SARAH, born in Madeira about 1839, residing in Edinburgh, 1851. [Census]

GRANT, WILLIAM, rector of the Scots College in Madrid, 1659-1665. [RSC.I.202]

GRANT, WILLIAM, born 1788, a merchant in Madeira, died 8 August 1866. [ARM]

GRANT, ..., son of William Grant, was born in Madeira on 22 December 1843. [W.V.435]

GRANT, Mrs, spouse of Patrick Grant a merchant in Baltimore, Maryland, and youngest daughter of Robert Gilmore a merchant there, died in Lisbon, Portugal, on 2 March 1805. [SM.67.325]

GRAY, ALEXANDER, a student at the Scots College in Rome, 1632. [RSC.I.109]

GRAY, ALEXANDER, a student at the Scots College in Rome, 1650. [RSC.I.114]

GRAY, CATHERINE, born 1797 in Turin, Italy, buried in Dundee Howff on 26 August 1822. [DCA.burial register]

SCOTS IN SOUTHERN EUROPE, 1600-1900

GRAY, GILBERT, a student at Padua University, Italy, in 1635. [RCPE]

GRAY, GILBERT, from Dunkeld, Perthshire, a student at the Scots College in Rome, 1657. [RSC.I.115]

GRAY, PATRICK, a student at the Scots College in Rome, 1650. [RSC.I.114]

GRAY, WILLIAM, from Angus, a student at the Scots College in Rome, 1608. [RSC.I.102]

GRAY, WILLIAM, from the Diocese of Brechin, a student at the Scots College in Rome, 1653, a monk in Germany, later a missionary in Scotland. [RSC.I.115]

GREGORIE, MARK, British Consul at Malaga, Spain, on 7 January 1789. [NRS.CE70.1.7]

GREGORSON, ALEXANDER, in Spain and Portugal, letters, 1805-1809. [NRS.NRAS.1285.box 1/7]

GREGORSON, ENEAS, in Spain, 1811. [NRS.NRAS.1285, box 1/1]; Assistant Commissary General to the British Forces, son of the late Angus Gregorson of Ardtorinish, Argyll, died in Portugal on 17 May 1813. [SM.75.557]

GREEN, JAMES S., born 1850, from Glasgow, died 11 March 1846, buried in the British Cemetery in Funchal, Madeira. [ARM]

GRONDISTON, ROBERT, from Fife, a student at the Scots College in Rome, 1610. [RSC.I.103]

GROSSET or MUIRHEAD, JAMES, of Breadisholm, Berwickshire, a merchant in Lisbon, Portugal, in 1766. [NRS.RS18.15.224]

SCOTS IN SOUTHERN EUROPE, 1600-1900

GROSSETT, DIANA, daughter of Walter Grossett, married Robert Walpole, HM Envoy-extraordinary and minister-plenipotentiary, in Lisbon, Portugal, on 8 May 1780. [SM.42.333]

GUILDMASTER, DANIEL, a merchant in Lisbon, Portugal, 1739. [NRS.AC9.6447; AC10.274]

GUILDMASTER, JOHN, a merchant in Lisbon, Portugal, in 1739. [NRS.AC9.6447; AC10.274]

GUNNING, Lieutenant General, Colonel of the 65th Regiment of Foot, brother of the late Duchess of Hamilton and Argyle, died in Naples, Italy, in 1797. [SM.59.782]

GUTHRIE, DAVID, from the Diocese of St Andrews, a student at the Scots College in Rome, 1672, a missionary in Scotland, died in Arbroath, Angus, on 9 March 1708. [RSC.I.118]

GUTHRIE, WILLIAM, born 4 August 1728 in the Diocese of Aberdeen, a student at the Scots College in Rome, 1750, died in Mortlach, Scotland, 1 May 1795. [RSC.I.136]

HACKET, ANDREW, born 1623, son of David Hacket and his wife Margaret Richardson in the Diocese of St Andrews, a student at the Scots College in Rome, 1701, died 21 May 1751. [RSC.I.125]

HAIG, BARBARA, in The Villa Haig, Rome, was served heir to her brother James Haig of Bemersyde, Berwickshire, a Writer to the Signet on 17 March 1858, [NRS.S/H]; an inventory, 1873. [NRS.SC70.164/527]

HAIG, MARY, from Bemersyde, Berwickshire, in Italy, was served heir to her brother James Haig of Bemersyde a Writer to

the Signet on 17 March 1858, [NRS.S/H]; dead by 1871.
[NRS.RD5.1417/304]

HAIG, SOPHIA, from Bemersyde, Berwickshire, in Italy, was
served heir to her brother James Haig of Bemersyde a Writer to
the Signet on 17 March 1858, [NRS.S/H]

HAIRSTON, JOHN, from Nithsdale, Dumfries-shire, a student
at the Scots College in Rome, 1610. [RSC.I.103]

HALIDAY, WILLIAM, a student at the Scots College in Rome,
in 1615. [RSC.I.104]

HALL, JOHN, a student at the Scots College in Rome, in 1677.
[RSC.I.119]

HALL, ROBERT, Lieutenant Colonel of the 37th Regiment of
Foot, died in Minorca, Spain, on 18 December 1763. [SM.26.55]

HALL, WILLIAM, born 1751, son of James Hall and his wife
Joan Reafin in the Diocese of Aberdeen, a student at the Scots
College in Rome, 1769, died in America. [RSC.I.141]

HAMILTON, Captain G., of the Royal Engineers, died in
Lisbon, Portugal, on 17 June 1810. [SM.72.559]

HAMILTON, ISAAC, from Aberdeen, a student at the Scots
College in Rome, 1612. [RSC.I.104]

HAMILTON, General JOHN, of Grange, in Portuguese Service,
testament, 1767. [Edinburgh Commissariat, NRS]

HAMILTON, MARY, born 1808, from Greenock, Renfrewshire,
died on Madeira on 17 September 1825. [ARM]

SCOTS IN SOUTHERN EUROPE, 1600-1900

HAMILTON, THOMAS, a student at the Scots College in Rome, in 1654. [RSC.I.115]

HAMILTON, THOMAS, born 1790, son of Professor William Hamilton and his wife Elizabeth Stirling, died in Pisa, Italy, on 7 December 1842, buried in Florence, Italy. [SGS]

HAMILTON, Sir WILLIAM, British Envoy to Naples, Italy, in 1796. [NRS.GD155.1216]

HAMILTON, WILLIAM, assistant surgeon to the 27th Regiment, son of James Hamilton of Braehead, died in Messina, Sicily, on 29 July 1806. [SM.67.887]

HAMILTON, Lady, wife of Sir William Hamilton, Knight of the Bath, British minister at the Royal Court of Naples, died in Naples, Italy, in August 1782. [SM.44.502]

HAMILTON, Mrs, of Dalzell, Lanarkshire, died in Cadiz, Spain, on 24 August 1824. [SM.94.511]

HAMILTON, ..., aboard The Defiance arrived in Madeira after a 3 week voyage, from England[?], with 6 or 7 weeks to get to Jamaica, a letter by .....Hamilton, possibly of the Royal Navy, dated 1711. [NRS.GD406.1.7336]

HARVEY, JAMES, son of Alexander Harvey and Mary Collinson in the Diocese of Aberdeen, a student at the Scots College in Rome, in 1718. [RSC.I.129]

HAY, EDWARD WILLIAM AURIOL DRUMMOND, Consul General in Tangier, died 28 February 1845, inventory, 1846, Comm. Edinburgh. [NRS]

HAY, GEORGE, born 24 August 1729 in the Diocese of Edinburgh, a student at the Scots College in Rome, 1751, died in

the seminary at Aquhortis, Scotland, 15 February 1811.
[RSC.I.137]

HAY, JAMES, a student at Padua University, Italy, in 1627.
[RCPE]

HAY, JAMES, a Jacobite in Urbino, Italy, in 1717. [JU]

HAY, JAMES RICHARDSON, of Seggieden, Perthshire, born
in 1804, died in 1854. [Protestant Cemetery in Rome, MI]

HAY, JOHN, a groom, a Jacobite in Urbino, Italy, in 1717. [JU]

HAY, JOHN, of Restalrig, a Writer to the Signet, a Jacobite in
1745, escaped to Italy. [P.1.295]

HAY, or COLINSON, WILLIAM, a student at the Scots
College in Rome, 1656. [RSC.I.115]

HAY, WILLIAM, of Edington, Berwickshire, alias Don
Guillielmo Hay, Captain in Spanish Service, a prisoner at
Berwick, 1747. [P.1.246]

HAY, WILLIAM, born 1750, son of James Hay and his wife
Joan Reafin in Aberdeenshire, a priest educated at the Scots
College in Rome, died in America. [RSC.I.141]

HAY, WILLIAM, possibly from Duns, Berwickshire, at
Talavera la Real, Spain, in 1809. [NRS.NRAS.2720. bundle 724]

HAY,......, daughter of Colonel Hay of the Banffshire Regiment,
was born in Gibraltar on 30 December 1801. [SM.64.181]

HAY, Mrs, Countess of Inverness, a Jacobite in Urbino, Italy,
1718. [JU]

SCOTS IN SOUTHERN EUROPE, 1600-1900

HAYNE, CHARLOTTE, born in Gibraltar about 1815, a stay-maker in Edinburgh by 1851. [Census]

HEGGAT, ARCHIBALD, a student at the Scots College in Rome, in 1622, later in Flanders. [RSC.I.106]

HEGGAT, GEORGE, from Glasgow, a student at the Scots College in Rome, in 1610. [RSC.I.103]

HENDERSON, ALEXANDER, son of ... Henderson a seedsman in Edinburgh, died in Oporto, Portugal, on 29 April 1814. [SM.76.638]

HENDERSON, ANNABELLA, in Florian, Malta, a testament, 1880. [NRS.RD5.2108/45/420]

HENDERSON, DAVID, born 1795, son of David Henderson and his wife Barbara Rutherford in Edinburgh, died in Naples, Italy, on 28 December 1824. [SGS]

HENDERSON, DAVID SMITH, in Rome, heir to his father William Low Henderson an architect and builder in Aberdeen who died 4 June 1899. [NRS.S/H]

HENDERSON, GEORGE, born 1837, formerly of the 1st Edinburgh Artisans, a volunteer under Garibaldi, in Italy in 1860. [SHR.57.175]

HENDERSON, JANE, born 1832, daughter of Dr William Henderson in Caskieben, Aberdeenshire, died 5 December 1866, buried in the British Cemetery in Funchal, Madeira. [ARM]

HENDERSON, NICHOLAS, in Naples, Italy, a letter, 1778. [NRS.GD172.478]

SCOTS IN SOUTHERN EUROPE, 1600-1900

HENDERSON, THOMAS, born 1802, son of George Henderson and Janet Tod, died in Leghorn (Livorno), Italy, on 11 October 1854. [Pittenweem, Fife, MI],

HENDERSON, WILLIAM, son of John Henderson of Caulfield and his wife Isabella Stuart in the Diocese of Moray, a student at the Scots College in Rome, in 1733. [RSC.I.132]

HENDERSON, WILLIAM, MD, from Leith, died in Madeira on 23 October 1834, inventory, 1835, Comm. Edinburgh. [NRS]

HENRY, JOSEPH, a student at the Scots College in Valladolid, Spain, in 1774, later in America. [RSC.I.206]

HEPBURN, PATRICK, a student at the Scots College in Rome, in 1602. [RSC.I.101]

HERRIES, CHARLES, a merchant in Barcelona, Spain, a bond, in 1768. [NRS.GD38.1.987]

HERRIES, JOHN, brother of Robert Herries, a student at the Scots College in Madrid, in 1734. [RSC.I.200]

HERRIES, NINA, daughter of Sir Robert Herries a banker in London, married Captain Foote of the Royal Navy, in Madrid on 22 January 1793. [SM.55.100]

HERRIES, ROBERT, son of John Herries of Auchensheen, a student at the Scots College in Madrid, 1722. [RSC.I.200]

HERVY, JAMES, a student at the Scots College in Rome, 1625. [RSC.I.107]

HEUGH, JOHN, born 1815, son of Reverend Hugh Heugh in Glasgow, educated in Glasgow University in 1830, died in d'Aquila, Italy, on 14 August 1893. [asgs]

SCOTS IN SOUTHERN EUROPE, 1600-1900

HEYWOOD, Mrs LUCINDA, wife of Henry Young in Madeira, died on 30 November 1808. [SM.71.237]

HILL, ROBERT TAWS, born 1859, youngest son of George H. Hill, died in San Remo, Italy, on 5 January 1880. [DCA#8257]

HODGE, DAVID, Deputy Consul at St Lucar, Spain, was admitted as a burgess and guilds-brother of Edinburgh, on 7 September 1757. [EBR]

HOG, THOMAS, a soldier, husband of Elizabeth Armour in Leith, killed in Tangiers in 1681. [South Leith Kirk Session Records, 8 September1681]

HOLDEN, RICHARD, son of Richard Gledhill Holden and his wife Mary Martin, died in Lisbon, Portugal, in 1886. [Bell Street MI, Dundee]

HOME, JOHN, Ensign of the 53rd Regiment, only son of Sir James Home of Manderston, Berwickshire, died in Gibraltar on 13 November 1765. [SM.27.671]

HOME, WILLIAM, a Scot aboard the Scots ship, the St James, before the Inquisition in the Canaries on 15 July 1591. ['The Inquisition in the Canaries', London, 1911]

HOME, WILLIAM, a merchant trading in the province of Guipuzcoa, Spain, 1591, [NRS.JC66.8]

HOME, WILLIAM, Earl of Home, Colonel of the 25th Regiment of Foot, a Lieutenant General, Governor of Gibraltar, Lord Lieutenant of Berwickshire, died in Gibraltar, 28 April 1761. [SM.23.279]

SCOTS IN SOUTHERN EUROPE, 1600-1900

HOME, the Earl of, married Miss Coutts, daughter of Mr Coutts a banker in London, in Italy during 1790. [SM.52.257]

HONYMAN, MUNGO, Assistant Commissary to the Forces, son of the late Patrick Honyman of Graemsay, died in Lisbon, Portugal, on 9 August 1809. [SM.71.718]

HOOD, ALEXANDER OGILVIE, born 1841, an English teacher, died 1 March 1905, buried in the British Cemetery in Funchal, Madeira. [ARM]

HOOME, Mrs, of Argary, wife of David Munro Binning, died in Madeira 'in the prime of life' on 29 May 1806. [SM.67.566]

HOPE, CHARLES, second son of Charles Hope commissioner at Chatham, died in Lisbon, Portugal, on 30 December 1805. [SM.67.79]

HOPE, J.A., in Malta, letters, 1890s. [NRS.GD377.328-329]

HORN, THOMAS, a merchant in Lisbon, Portugal, was admitted as a burgess and guilds-brother of Edinburgh, on 14 February 1753. [EBR]

HORNER, FRANCIS, born 12 August 1778, son of John Horner a linen merchant in Edinburgh, died in Pisa, Italy, on 8 February 1817. [SGS]

HOSSACK, EUPHEMIA, born in Gibraltar about 1829, a house servant in Edinburgh by 1851. [Census]

HOURIE, JOHN CHARLES, of Xerris, Spain, was admitted as a burgess and guilds-brother of Ayr on 28 February 1791. [ABR]

HOUSTON, JAMES, born in Cardross, Dunbartonshire, died in Rome on 18 August 1924. [Protestant Cemetery in Rome, MI]

SCOTS IN SOUTHERN EUROPE, 1600-1900

HOUSTON, JOHN, Captain of <u>HMS Vestal</u>, died in Lisbon, Portugal, in November 1810. [SM.73.153]

HOUSTON, WILLIAM, born 1788, a Lieutenant of the 71st Regiment, only son of Hugh Houston of Creich, Sutherland, was killed at Almeida, Spain, on 5 May 1811. [SM.73.558]

HOUSTON, Lieutenant Colonel, of the Rifle Corps, died in Gibraltar in 1800. [SM.63.72]

HOWISON, WILLIAM, minister of Cambusnethan, Lanarkshire, died in Madeira on 24 July 1780. [SM.42.505]

HUME, Captain JOHN, married Joanna Stirling, only daughter of Lieutenant Colonel James Stirling of the 42nd Regiment, in Gibraltar on 21 October 1807. [SM.70.235]

HUME, THOMAS, from the Lothians, a student at the Scots College in Rome, 1613. [RSC.I.104]

HUNTER, JAMES, a Scots agent in Spain, 1580s

HUNTER, JOHN, a merchant in St Lucar, was admitted as a burgess and guilds-brother of Ayr on 27 July 1776. [ABR]; consul in Cadiz, a letter, 18 May 1784. [NRS.GD113.4.157]; married Margaret Congalton, eldest daughter of Dr Charles Congalton a physician, in Edinburgh on 27 December 1787. [SM.49.620]

HUNTER, JOHN, eldest son of Robert Hunter a merchant in Paisley, Renfrewshire, died in Madeira on 5 December 1786. [SM.49.50]

HUNTER, JOHN M., a merchant from Glasgow, died in Malaga, Spain, on 17 September 1820. [SM.86.479]

SCOTS IN SOUTHERN EUROPE, 1600-1900

HUNTER, MARY GREY, third daughter of the late General Sir Martin Hunter, GCMG, of Anton's Hill, Berwickshire, died in Rome on 14 February 1855. [Protestant Cemetery in Rome, MI]

HUNTER, ROBERT, of the Hunter of Hunterston family, resident in Naples, Italy, in 17...., [NRS.GD52.1536]

HUNTER, ROBERT HEPBURNE SWINTON, of Hafton, Argyll, born in Edinburgh on 3 April 1860, died in Rome on 28 January 1904. [Protestant Cemetery in Rome, MI]

HUNTER, WILLIAM FREDERICK, of Hafton, Argyll, born 19 January 1841, advocate and barrister at law, died 29 April 1880, 'buried in the English Cemetery of Madeira'. [Dunoon MI, Bute]

HUNTER, Mrs, spouse of John Hunter HM Consul for San Lucar and Seville, died at San Lucar de Barameda in Spain on 29 October 1791. [SM.53.569]

HUNTER, ..., son of Lieutenant Colonel Hunter of the 48th Regiment, was born in Gibraltar on 14 January 1800. [SM.62.288]

HUTCHISON, HUGH, born 1845, son of John Hutchison a merchant in Funchal, Madeira, died 16 September 1866, buried in the British Cemetery in Funchal. [ARM]

HUTCHISON, JAMES ANDERSON, an artist of Woodlands, Lochgilphead, Argyll, died in Rome on 27 February 1882. [Protestant Cemetery in Rome, MI]

HUTCHIESON, MATTHEW, surgeon on the Medical Staff, died in Gibraltar on 13 August 1804. [SM.66.885]

HUTCHESON, STEWART SMITH, a merchant in Oporto, Portugal, was served heir to his aunt Ann Elizabeth Hutcheson in

Fairlie, Largs, Ayrshire, who died 4 May 1868, on 10 November 1868. [NRS.S/H]

HUTTON, JAMES, from Dumfries, a student at Padua University, Italy, in 1677. [RCPE]

INGLIS, CATHERINE ANNE, eldest daughter of William Inglis of Middleton, married Edward Henry Shenley a Captain of the Rifle Brigade, in Leghorn, [Livorno], Italy, on 17 August 1823. [SM.92.310]

INNES, CHARLES, born 1694, son of Francis Innes and his wife Joan Metlin in Aberdeen, a student at the Scots College in Rome, 1710. [RSC.I.127]

INNES, GEORGE, son of Colonel James Innes and his wife ... Maxwell, a student at the Scots College in Valladolid, Spain, in 1664, died in 26 February 1698. [RSC.I.199]

INNES, JOHN, a student at Padua University, Italy, in 1722. [RCPE]

INNES, MARION L., daughter of Robert Innes and his wife Sarah Marshall, was born 22 July 1809 and baptised in the Anglican Church of Madeira on 5 November 1809. [ARM]; died there on 14 April 1810. [ARM]

INNES, ROBERT, born 1771, died on Madeira 14 December 1813. [ARM]; a deed, 2 December 1799. [NRS.RD4.270.692]

INNES, ROBERT, son of Robert Innes and his wife Sarah Gilbert, was born 26 October 1810 and baptised in the Anglican Church of Madeira on 8 November1810. [ARM]

INNES, ROBERT, born in Madeira around 1811, a sugar commission agent in Edinburgh by 1851, with his daughters

SCOTS IN SOUTHERN EUROPE, 1600-1900

Margaret, born in Madeira in 1841, and Agnes born in Madeira in 1846. [Census]

INNES, SARAH, born in 1783, died and was buried in the British Cemetery, Funchal, Madeira, on 6 January 1853. [ARM]

INNES, SARAH WOOD, born 1844, daughter of Robert Innes a merchant in Madeira, died and was buried in the British Cemetery, Funchal, Madeira, on 28 July 1845. [ARM]

INNES, WALTER, from the Diocese of Aberdeen, a student at the Scots College in Rome, 1681, died 15 August 1722. [RSC.I.121]

INNES, Lieutenant WILLIAM, of the 94th Regiment, eldest son of James Innes of Kerse, died in Cadiz, Spain, on 11 July 1810. [SM.72.718]

IRVIN, ALEXANDER, a student at the Scots College in Rome, 1650. [RSC.I.114]

IRVINE, ALEXANDER, in Rome, 1817. [NRS.NRAS.1500, bundle104]

IRVIN, CHRISTOPHER, a student at the Scots College in Rome, 1643. [RSC.I.112]

IRVINE, JAMES, youngest son of Alexander Irvine of Drum, Aberdeenshire, died in Rome on 11 December 1831. [AJ#4382]; James Irvine of Drum, Aberdeenshire, a historical painter, member of the Royal Institution of Edinburgh, and of the Academy of Fine Art, born in Aberdeen on 28 March 1759, died in Rome on 11 December 1831. [Protestant Cemetery in Rome, MI]

SCOTS IN SOUTHERN EUROPE, 1600-1900

IRVIN, JOHN, from Aberdeen, a student at the Scots College in Rome, 1652, later a Jesuit, died in Germany. [RSC.I.115]

IRVIN, JOHN, of Hilton, born 1633, from the Diocese of Aberdeen, a student at the Scots College in Rome, 1659, chaplain to the French Ambassador in 1668, brother-in-law of the Marquis of Bagni. [RSC.I.116]

IRVIN, JOHN, of Belty, a student at the Scots College in Rome, 1662, later in Paris. [RSC.I.117]

IRVIN, JOHN, born 1652, a student at the Scots College in Rome, 1671, a missionary in Scotland, died at Gordon Castle, Aberdeenshire, on 19 April 1717. [RSC.I.118]

IRVINE, Mrs MATILDA, relict of Dr William Irvine physician to the forces in Sicily and Malta, died 10 October 1833. [St Cuthbert's MI. Edinburgh]

IRVIN, ROBERT, a student at the Scots College in Rome, 1639. [RSC.I.111]

IRVIN, ROBERT, born 1630 in Aberdeen, son of Alexander Irvine and Mary Menzies his wife, a student at the Scots College in Valladolid, Spain, 1648, later at the Scots College in Rome. [RSC.I.198]

IRVINE, Dr WILLIAM, an army physician, son of the late Dr Irvine of Glasgow University, died in Malta on 23 March 1811. [SM.73.637]

IRVING, GEORGE, born 1763, son of John Irving a farrier and his wife Agnes Johnston in Annan, Dumfries-shire, a merchant, died in Messina, Italy, on 20 August 1817. [SGS]

SCOTS IN SOUTHERN EUROPE, 1600-1900

JACKSON, JOHN, a student at the Scots College in Rome, 1657. [RSC.I.116]

JAMESON, JAMES WARDROPE, in Genoa, Italy, son of William Jameson and his wife Elizabeth Jane Turnbull in Portobello, Midlothian, 1851. [NRS.S/H]

JAMESON, JOHN, born 1659, from Aberdeen, a student at the Scots College in Rome, 1677, died in Edinburgh on 20 March 1700. [RSC.I.119]

JAMIESON, JOHN, born 1831, son of John Jamieson in Glasgow, died 26 November 1850, buried in the British Cemetery, Funchal, Madeira. [ARM]

JANNETTI, FRANCESCO, a teacher of Italian in Edinburgh, died in Turin, Italy, on 12 September 1855, inventory, 1855, Comm. Edinburgh. [NRS]

JARDINE, ALEXANDER, Colonel of the Artillery, British Consul in Corunna, Spain, testament, 15 September 1800, Commissariat of Edinburgh. [SRS]

JARDINE, HENRY, born 12 March 1803, son of Sir Henry Jardine and his wife Catherine Skene, from Midlothian, died in Rome on 11 January 1840. [Protestant Cemetery in Rome, MI][SGS]

JOHNSON, WILLIAM, a partner of the firm Newton, Gordon and Johnson in Madeira from 1775. [ARM]

JOHNSTON, ARCHIBALD, surgeon in the Royal Navy, died Lisbon, Portugal, on 22 December 1843, an inventory, 1847, Comm. Edinburgh. [NRS]

SCOTS IN SOUTHERN EUROPE, 1600-1900

JOHNSTONE, GEORGE, born in 1804, son of Lieutenant Colonel Johnstone of the 58th Regiment, died in Malta in 1805. [SM.67.967]

JOHNSTONE, GEORGE, Colonel of the 58th Regiment, died in Messina, Sicily, on 28 July 1806. [SM.67.807]

JOHNSTONE, GEORGE, born in Earlston, Berwickshire, 2 November 1780, son of Reverend Laurence Johnstone and his wife Esther Lauriston, staff surgeon of the Connaught Rangers, died in Corfu, Greece, in 1833. [F.2.149]

JOHNSTON, JAMES, born 1797, youngest son of the late Walter Johnston in Joppa, Portobello, died at Leghorn, [Livorno], Italy, on 20 May 1817. [SM.79.480]

JOHNSTON, NICOLAS, a student at the Scots College in Rome, 1641. [RSC.I.112]

JOHNSTON, PATRICK, a student at the Scots College in Rome, 1622. [RSC.I.106]

JOHNSTONE, SOPHIA, wife of Francis Platamone, Count of St Antonio, son of the Duke of Cannezzaro, Sicily, was granted the lands of Leaston and of Friars Carse in Scotland, in 1815. [NRS.RGS.151.8; 152.26]

JOHNSTON, THOMAS, born 1618 in Aberdeen, son of Robert and Agnes Johnston, a student at the Scots College at Madrid, Spain, 1647, later a monk at the Scots Monastery at Ratisbon, Germany, died 17 December 1663. [RSC.I.196]

JOHNSTON, WILLIAM, a student at the Scots College in Rome, in 1654. [RSC.I.115]

SCOTS IN SOUTHERN EUROPE, 1600-1900

JOHNSTON, Commander, married Charlotte Dee in Lisbon, Portugal, on 31 January 1781. [SM.44.110]

JULIAN, ELEANOR, born 1792, wife of David Maitland Makgill of Rankeillor in Fife, died on Madeira 9 January 1823. [ARM]

KAY, ROBERT, a Major in Portuguese Service, married Margaret Donaldson, youngest daughter of the late William Donaldson of Manbean, in Elgin, Moray, on 17 March 1814. [SM.76.318]

KEIR, WILLIAM, Captain of Horse at Tangier and later of the garrison at Tangier, relict Katherine Millar, parents of Elizabeth, Margaret, and William, deeds, 1686, 1687. [NRS.RD2.67.263; RD3.66.187/361]

KEIR, WILLIAM, from Aberdeen, a student at the Scots College in Rome, 1602. [RSC.I.101]

KEITH, GEORGE, 9th Earl Marischal, in Madrid, Spain, in 1737, a letter. [NRS.CH12.12.933]

KENNEDY, ALEXANDER, a student at the Scots College in Rome, 1613. [RSC.I.104]

KENNEDY, ALEXANDER, born 1736, from the Diocese of Dunkeld, a student at the Scots College in Rome, 1759, died in Arisaig, Scotland, 11 July 1773. [RSC.I.138]

KENNEDY, DAVID, of Kirkmichael, died in Florence, Italy, on 1 September 1833, inventory, 1836, Comm. Edinburgh. [NRS]

KENNEDY, GEORGE, Royal Navy, died in Rome on 19 October 1841, inventory, 1842, Comm. Edinburgh. [NRS]

SCOTS IN SOUTHERN EUROPE, 1600-1900

KENNEDY, HUGH, a student at Padua University, Italy, in 1666. [RCPE]

KENNEDY, JAMES, born 1660, from the Diocese of Aberdeen, a student at the Scots College in Rome, 1693, died in Glenlivet, Banffshire, on 6 June 1704. [RSC.I.122]

KER, ALEXANDER, Captain of the 43rd Regiment of Foot, son of James Ker of Blackshiels, died at Lumiar near Lisbon, Portugal, on 2 April 1809. [SM.71.398]

KERR, HENRY, born 1702, from Graden, Teviotdale, an officer of the Spanish Army from 1722 to 1728, returned to Scotland in 1745 to fight for the Jacobites, was captured and banished from Scotland in 1748, died in 1751. [NRS.NRAS#NA6719]; Henry Ker of Graden, a Lieutenant Colonel in Spanish Service, died at St Lucar, Spain on 22 December 1751. [SM.13.53]

KERR, JOHN, from Lauden, a student at the Scots College in Rome, 1602. [RSC.I.101]

KERR, JOHN, of Dalmuir House, Glasgow, born 1788, died in Rome on 3 April 1848. [Protestant Cemetery in Rome, MI]

KERR, ..., daughter of James Kerr an analytical chemist, was born at Pueblo Nueva, Tharsis Mines, Huelva, Spain, on 19 January 1885. [S#12963]

KER, ..., daughter of William Herries Ker, was born in Rome on 20 January 1824. [SM.93.382]

KEVAN, WILLIAM, born 1812, a merchant in Glasgow, died in Madeira on 17 December 1840. [W#II/106]

KILSYTH, Viscount, a Jacobite in Urbino, Italy, in 1717. [JU]

SCOTS IN SOUTHERN EUROPE, 1600-1900

KINCAID, CLEMENT, from Edinburgh, a student at the Scots College in Rome, 1614. [RSC.I.104]

KINCAID, PATRICK, a merchant in Cadiz, Spain, in 1790; bought the lands of Knockincurr, 3 July 1784. [NRS.RS.Wigtown#245; RGS.122.112]

KINGSTON, Viscount, a Jacobite in Urbino, Italy, in 1717. [JU]

KINLAY, WILLIAM, born 1807, from Kirkintilloch, Lanarkshire, died and was buried in the British Cemetery, Funchal, Madeira, on 6 October 1844. [ARM]

KINNAIRD, LAURA, died in Madeira in April 1810. [SM.72.479]

KINNEAR, JAMES, a Writer to the Signet, born 22 December 1822, died in Cadiz, Spain, on 21 June 1849, buried in the Protestant burial ground there. [St John's, Edinburgh, MI]

KING, THOMAS, son of David King and his wife Janet Forbes in Hillbrae, a traveller in Poland who died in Saintsoi, Italy, on October 1600. [MSC.II.55]

KINLOCH, THOMAS, in Gibraltar, 1785. [NRS.GD1.931.105]

KINNAIRD, LAURA, died on Madeira 20 March 1810. [ARM]

KIRKPATRICK, HARRIET, daughter of the late William Kirkpatrick of Conheath, died at Adra, Spain, on 29 February 1824. [SM.93.639]

KIRKPATRICK MARIA MANUELA, second daughter of William Kirkpatrick in Malaga, Spain, married Count de Montijo, moved to Paris with her children in 1834. She died in Madrid during 1879. [WKM]

SCOTS IN SOUTHERN EUROPE, 1600-1900

KIRKPATRICK, MARIQUITA MALVINA, eldest daughter of William Kirkpatrick in Malaga, Spain, married Cipiano Palafox, Count Jeva, in Malaga in 1818. [SM.82.103]

KIRKPATRICK, THOMAS JAMES, in Malaga, Spain, married Carlotta Kirkpatrick, second daughter of William Kirkpatrick, in Gibraltar, 1818. [SM.82.103]

KIRKPATRICK, WILLIAM, of Conheath, a merchant in Malaga, Spain, in 1788, husband of Francisca de Grivegnee y Gallegos, American Consul in Malaga pre 1812. [WKM]

LAMB, ANDREW, from Hamilton, Lanarkshire, a student at the Scots College in Rome, 1610. [RSC.I.103]

LAMBTON, Lady SUSAN, wife of General Lambton and sister of the Earl of Strathmore, died in Nice, France, on 26 February 1769. [SM.31.166]

LAMOND, PETER, born around 1797 son of Peter Lamond and Elizabeth Colville his wife in Edinburgh, died in Corfu, Greece, on 4 August 1842. [SGS]

LANDEL, DAVID, from Glasgow, a student at the Scots College in Rome, in 1624. [RSC.I.107]

LANDEL, ROBERT, a student at the Scots College in Rome in 1616. [RSC.I.105]

LANG, JOHN SIBBALD, an Ensign of the 94th Regiment, second son of the late John Lang sheriff clerk of Selkirkshire, was killed at the storming of Badajoz, Spain, on 6 April 1812. [SM.74.479]

SCOTS IN SOUTHERN EUROPE, 1600-1900

LANG, WILLIAM, from Aberdeen, a student at the Scots College in Madrid, Spain, in 1643, later in the service of the Marchioness de Costello Rodriguez. [RSC.I.195]

LAURENCE, GEORGE, from Edinburgh, a student at the Scots College in Rome, 1613. [RSC.I.104]

LAURIE, WILLIAM WILSON, a merchant from Leith, by Edinburgh, died at Capri, near Naples, Italy, on 15 June 1857, inventory, 1857, Comm. Edinburgh. [NRS]

LAUTENS {?}, HUGH, from Edinburgh, a student at Padua University, Italy, in 1627. [RCPE]

LAW, JOHN, a volunteer under Garibaldi in Italy, 1860. [SHR.57.176]

LAWRIE, SARAH A., born 1839, from Dalkeith, Midlothian, died and was buried in the British Cemetery, Funchal, Madeira, on 3 July 1872. [ARM]

LAWRIE, Major, of the 79th Regiment of Foot, eldest son of Andrew Lawrie an army agent, died at Burges, Spain, on 23 September 1812. [SM.74.886]

LEATHAM, Captain, of the 4TH Dragoon Guards, eldest son of Lieutenant Colonel Leatham of George Square, Edinburgh, died at Elvas, Spain, on 2 September 1812. [SM.74.806]

LEITH, ALEXANDER, a student at the Scots College in Rome, 1642. [RSC.I.112]

LEITH, ALEXANDER, a student at the Scots College in Rome, 1651, died as a Jesuit missionary in Scotland. [RSC.I.114]

SCOTS IN SOUTHERN EUROPE, 1600-1900

LEITH, GEORGE, from Aberdeen, a student at the Scots College in Rome, 1634, later Rector of the Scots College in Paris. [RSC.I.110]

LEITH, JAMES ALEXANDER WELLESLEY, born 1835, son of Sir Alexander Wellesly Leith in Edinburgh, died in Gibraltar on 21 February 1857. [SGS]

LEITH, PATRICK, born 1688, son of Patrick Leith of Harthill and his wife Joan Ogilvy in Aberdeen, a student at the Scots College in Rome, 1712, died in London 5 May 1760. [RSC.I.128]

LEITH, Sir WELLESLEY, born 1807 in Edinburgh, died in Funchal, Madeira, on 4 April 1842. [SGS]

LESLIE, ANDREW, from Moray, a student at the Scots College in Rome, 1618, a Jesuit missionary, died in Scotland. [RSC.I.106]

LESLIE, ANDREW, a student at the Scots College in Rome, 1638. [RSC.I.111]

LESLIE, ERNEST, born 5 February 1713, son of Charles Leslie and his wife Elizabeth Fordyce, a student at the Scots College in Madrid, Spain, in 1722. [RSC.I.200]

LESLY, GEORGE, from Aberdeen, a student at the Scots College in Rome, 1608. [RSC.I.102]

LESLIE, HENRY, from Ulster, a student at Padua University, Italy, in 1715. [RCPE]

LESLIE, JAMES, born 10 May 1703, son of John Leslie and his wife Joan Gordon, in the Diocese of Aberdeen, a student at the Scots College in Rome, 1721. [RSC.I.129]

SCOTS IN SOUTHERN EUROPE, 1600-1900

LESLIE, JOHN, from Moray, a student at the Scots College in Rome, 1618, died as a Jesuit missionary in Scotland. [RSC.I.106]

LESLIE, ROBERT, born 1802, died in Rome on 21 June 1827. [Protestant Cemetery in Rome, MI]

LESLY, WILLIAM, from Aberdeen, a student at the Scots College in Rome, 1608. [RSC.I.102]

LESLY, WILLIAM, a student at the Scots College in Rome, 1615. [RSC.I.104]

LESLIE, WILLIAM, born 1605, from Aberdeen, a student at the Scots College in Rome, died 17 August 1698. [RSC.I.108]

LESLIE, WILLIAM, from the Diocese of Moray, a student at the Scots College in Rome, 1641. [RSC.I.111]

LESLIE, WILLIAM, son of William Leslie of Warthill, from the Diocese of Aberdeen, a student at the Scots College in Rome, 1675, later in Hungary, died 1727. [RSC.I.119]

LEWIS, or SANTORO, INA CATHERINE, daughter of Reverend George Lewis from Dundee and his wife Mary Anne Elizabeth Miller, died during 1888 in Rome. [Protestant Cemetery in Rome, MI]

LEWIS, JAMES, DD, born in Glasgow during 1805, a minister of the Free Church of Scotland in Leith and in Rome, died in Rome during 1872. [Protestant Cemetery in Rome, MI]

LEWIS, SARAH, born 24 May 1854, from Edinburgh, died 4 April 1930. [Protestant Cemetery in Rome, MI]

LIDDELL, GEORGE, in Lisbon, Portugal, probate, 1672, PCC

SCOTS IN SOUTHERN EUROPE, 1600-1900

LINDO, ANDREAS, a mariner aboard the <u>St Antonio of Leghorn</u>, [Livorno], Italy, in 1712. [NRS.AC9.428]

LINDSAY, HENRY, from Brechin, Angus, a student at the Scots College in Rome, 1623, later a Jesuit. [RSC.I.107]

LINDSAY, ROBERT, son of Lieutenant General James Lindsay, died in Genoa, Italy, on 18 December 1856. [Balcarres, Fife, MI]

LINLITHGOW, the Earl of, a Jacobite in Urbino, Italy, in, 1717. [JU]

LISLE, ROBERT, Captain of the 97th Regiment, died in Corfu, Greece, on 14 November 1843, inventory, 1844, Comm. Edinburgh. [NRS]

LISTON, ROBERT, in Madrid, Spain, letters, 1784. [NRS.GD253.145.8]

LITT, THOMAS, a merchant from Glasgow, died in Madeira on 24 February 1821; testament, 1823, Comm. Dumfries. [NRS]

LITTLE, ARCHIBALD, a merchant in Teneriffe, Canary Islands, son of Matthew Little a merchant in Langholm, 1794. [NRS.S/H]

LIVINGSTONE, E., in Trieste, letter, 1798. [NRS.GD51.1.532]

LIVINGSTONE, Captain FRANCIS, son of the late Sir Alexander Livingstone of Westquarter and Bedlomie, died in Lisbon on 11 October 1812. [SM.74.967]

LIVINGSTONE, JAMES, a student at the Scots College in Rome, 1678. [RSC.I.120]

SCOTS IN SOUTHERN EUROPE, 1600-1900

LIVINGSTONE, Captain JAMES, master of the Antonio of Leghorn, 1714. [NRS.AC8.175; 9.399]

LIVINGSTONE, JAMES, Earl of Linlithgow and of Callander, a Jacobite in 1715, fled to the continent in 1716, settled in Avignon and Urbino, died in Rome 1723. [JCR.43]

LOCKHART, ESTHER, daughter of the late Sir Alexander Macdonald Lockhart, died in Madeira on 3 April 1817. [SM.79.584]

LOCKHART of LEE, Count JAMES, General in the service of, and one of the Chamberlains to his Imperial Majesty, died in Pisa on 6 February 1790. He was succeeded by his eldest son Charles as a Count of the Holy Roman Empire and to his estates in Scotland. [SM.52.102]

LOCKHART, JAMES, youngest son of the late Count Lockhart of Lee, died in Pisa on 7 April 1790. [SM.52.205]

LOGIE, CHARLES, Consul General in Morocco, was admitted as a burgess of Montrose in 1796. [MBR]

LOGIE, GEORGE, British consul in Algiers, 1733. [NRS.CS228.B.2.53]

LORIMER, JAMES, master of the James of Crawfordsdyke, from Glasgow to the Canaries in January 1695, arrived in March, sailed from Tenerife with a cargo of Madeira wine bound for Glasgow, taken by a St Malo privateer on18 April, cargo and most of crew was captured, three crew left on board with privateers, the vessel was anchored at Mount Bay, Cornwall, after privateers had abandoned ship, then it was looted and wrecked by local Cornish men. [GA.TD1619/82]

SCOTS IN SOUTHERN EUROPE, 1600-1900

LOTHIAN, JAMES, from the Diocese of St Andrews, a student at the Scots College in Rome, 1631. [RSC.I.109]

LOUGHMAN, L., in Madeira, a deed of factory, 10 April 1790. [NRS.RD2.248.926]

LUMSDANE, ALEXANDER, from Aberdeen, a student at the Scots College in Rome, 1645, later a Dominican missionary in Scotland, possibly died in London. [RSC.I.113]

LUMSDANE, THOMAS, from Aberdeen, a student at the Scots College in Rome, 1644, a missionary in Scotland, Professor of Divinity in Paris, died there on 28 June 1671. [RSC.I.113]

LUNARDI, VINCENT, of Lucca, (the aeronaut), a burgess and guilds-brother of Edinburgh, 12 October 1785. [Edinburgh Burgess Roll]

LUNDIE, Reverend MARSHALL, BD, born 1857, fourth son of W. H. Lundie, a teacher in Auchterarder, Perthshire, died at Tharais Mines, Calanas, Spain, on 4 December 1884. [S#12919]

LUTFOOT, JAMES, a student at Padua University, 1700. [RCPE]

LYON, JOHN, Earl of Strathmore, died at sea on 7 March 1776 when bound for Lisbon 'for the recovery of his health'. [SM.38.163]

MACALISTER Captain DONALD, of Loup and Torresdale, born 1790, died in Florence on 10 December 1824. [SM.94.767]

MACALISTER, Mrs MARY, born 1793, wife of the late John MacAlister of Strathaird, Skye, died in Rome on 27 January 1869. [Protestant Cemetery in Rome, MI]

SCOTS IN SOUTHERN EUROPE, 1600-1900

MACAULAY, ALEXANDER, Treasurer of Malta, died there in 1805. [SM.67.566]

MACAULAY, GEORGE, a student at Padua University, 1736. [RCPE]

MACBEAN, WILLIAM, son of William MacBean, born in Leghorn on 12 December 1822, died 12 August 1842. [St John's, Edinburgh, MI]

MACBEAN, ..., son of Mrs MacBean, was born in Malta on 4 May 1813. [SM.75.638]

MACBRECK, JOHN, a student at the Scots College in Rome, 1617, later a Jesuit. [RSC.I.105]

MACBRECK, PATRICK, from Strathearn, a student at the Scots College in Rome, 1610. [RSC.I.103]

MACCALLUM, DONALD, born 1834, formerly of the 4th Battalion of the 60th Royal Rifles, a volunteer under Garibaldi, 1860. [SHR.57.175]

MCCARTNEY, JANE M., born 1806, from Kirkcudbrightshire, died 24 August 1824, buried in the British Cemetery in Funchal, Madeira. [ARM]

MACDONALD, AENEAS, born 1726 in the diocese of Lismore, a student at the Scots College in Rome,1740. [RSC.I.134]

MACDONALD, ALAN, son of Alexander MacDonald of Stonybridge and his wife Ziles MacDonald in the Diocese of the Isles, a student the Scots College in Rome, 1715, later rector of the Scots College in Valladolid, Spain, 1771, died in Scotland 1778. [RSC.I.128/205]

SCOTS IN SOUTHERN EUROPE, 1600-1900

MACDONALD, ALAN, son of Aeneas MacDonald of Scotus and his wife Florence MacLeod in the Diocese of Inverness, a student at the Scots College in Rome, 1721. [RSC.I.130]

MACDONALD, ALAN, born 1742 in the diocese of the Isles, a student at the Scots College in Rome, 1757, died in America. [RSC.I.138]

MACDONALD, ALEXANDER, born 1720, son of Aeneas MacDonald and his wife Anna MacDonald in the diocese of the Isles, a student at the Scots College in Rome, 1738. [RSC.I.133]

MACDONALD, ALEXANDER, born 1725 in the diocese of the Isles, a student at the Scots College in Rome, 1743. [RSC.I.135]

MACDONALD, ALEXANDER, born 16 February 1739 in Rome, son of Colin Erskine and Agatha Gigli, a student at the Scots College in Rome, 1748, died in Paris, 1811. [RSC.I.135]

MACDONALD, ALEXANDER, born 1736 in the diocese of the Isles, a student at the Scots College in Rome, 1754, died in Scotland, 1791. [RSC.I.137]

MACDONALD, ALEXANDER, son of John MacDonald and his wife Catharine MacDonald in the Diocese of the Isles, a student at the Scots College in Rome, 1770, died in the East Indies. [RSC.I.142]

MACDONALD, ALEXANDER, at the Scots College in Paris, in 1770 a student at the Scots College in Valladolid, Spain, 1775, a priest in Scotland, later in America. [RSC.I.205/206]

MACDONALD, ALEXANDER, son of Lachlan MacDonald and Isabella MacDonald, born in May 1758 in the Diocese of the Isles, a student at the Scots College in Rome, 1772. [RSC.I.143]

94

SCOTS IN SOUTHERN EUROPE, 1600-1900

MACDONALD, ALEXANDER, aged 21, a Lieutenant of the 92nd Regiment, second son of Major MacDonald of Dalchosnie, died in Vittoria, Spain, on 5 October 1813 from would received in battle in the Pyrenees on 25 July 1813. [SM.75.959]

MACDONALD, ALEXANDER R., died in Rome during 1878. [Protestant Cemetery in Rome, MI]

MACDONALD, ALLAN, a student at the Scots College in Valladolid, Spain, 1785, died 8 September 1793 in Edinburgh. [RSC.I.209]

MACDONALD, ANGUS, a student at the Scots College in Valladolid, Spain, 1771. [RSC.I.206]

MACDONALD, ANGUS, from Retland, a student at the Scots College in Valladolid, Spain, 1776, died 14 April 1784. [RSC.I.207]

MACDONALD, ANGUS, Major in the service of Portugal and of Great Britain died in Lisbon on 2April 1819. [SM.83.481]

MACDONALD, ARCHIBALD, a student at the Scots College in Valladolid, Spain, 1771, died 1813. [RSC.I.206]

MACDONALD, AUGUSTINE, born 1744 in the diocese of the Isles, a student at the Scots College in Rome, 1757, died in America. [RSC.I.138]

MACDONALD, AUGUSTINE, a student at the Scots College in Valladolid, Spain, 1771, ordained in 1780, a missionary in Strathdon, died at Scalan 1782. [RSC.I.206]

SCOTS IN SOUTHERN EUROPE, 1600-1900

MACDONALD, CHARLES, born 1773, a student at the Scots College in Valladolid, Spain, 1788, ordained 1798, a missionary in Knoydart, died 8 October 1848. [RSC.I.210]

MACDONALD, DONALD, a student at the Scots College in Valladolid, 1771. [RSC.I.206]

MACDONALD, DUGALD, born December 1719, son of Dugald MacDonald and his wife Catherine MacLean in the diocese of the Isles, a student at the Scots College in Rome, 1738. [RSC.I.133]

MACDONALD, EVAN, a student at the Scots College in Valladolid, Spain, 1788, ordained in 1800, priest at Braemar. [RSC.I.210]

MACDONALD, FRANCIS, son of Donald MacDonald and Christina MacDonald, a student at the Scots College in Rome, 1768. [RSC.I.141]

MACDONALD, JAMES, born 1736, in the Diocese of the Isles, a student at the Scots College in Rome, 1754, died on Prince Edward Island, Canada, 1786. [RSC.I.137]

MACDONALD, JAMES, born in 1743, died 1 August 1766. [Protestant Cemetery in Rome, MI]; Sir James MacDonald, died in Ro
me on 26 July 1766.' He was the first Protestant that had a public funeral in that country'. He was succeeded in estate and titles by his only brother Alexander, an officer in the footguards. [SM.28.436]

MACDONALD, JOHN, born 1691, son of Alexander MacDonald of Inverlair and his wife Christine MacDonald in the Diocese of Lochaber, a student at the Scots College in Rome, 1713, died 25 December 1761. [RSC.I.128]

SCOTS IN SOUTHERN EUROPE, 1600-1900

MACDONALD, JOHN, born 1727 in the Diocese of the Isles, a student at the Scots College, 1743, died 1779. [RSC.I.135]

MACDONALD, JOHN, born 1750 in Torbreck, Inverness-shire, died in Madeira on 5 July 1811. [ARM]

MACDONALD, JOHN, Colonel of the King of Portugal's Guards, was granted the lands of Letham on 6 August 1771. [NRS.C3.20.55]

MACDONALD, JOHN, born 1752, a student at the Scots College in Valladolid, 1771, a missionary in Scotland from 1784, died in Arisaig on 8 July 1834. [RSC.I.205]

MACDONALD, JOHN, a student at the Scots College in Valladolid, Spain, 1785, died in Scotland. [RSC.I.209]

MACDONALD, JOHN, a student at the Scots College in Valladolid, Spain, 1788, later in America. [RSC.I.210]

MACDONALD, LAURENCE, born in Gask, Perthshire, on 14 February 1798, a sculptor, died in Rome on 4 March 1878. [Protestant Cemetery in Rome, MI]

MACDONALD, REGINALD, son of Aeneas MacDonald and his wife Catharine MacGregor, a student at the Scots College in Rome, 1738. [RSC.I.133]

MACDONALD, REGINALD, son of James MacDonald and his wife Isabella MacDonel in the Diocese of the Isles, a student at the Scots College in Rome, 1769. [RSC.I.141]

MACDONALD, RODERICK, born 1761, a student at the Scots College in Valladolid, Spain, 1780, ordained 1791, died 29 September 1828. [RSC.I.209]

SCOTS IN SOUTHERN EUROPE, 1600-1900

MACDONALD, RONALD, born 1754, a student at the Scots College in Valladolid, 1771, a missionary from 1780, died in Morar, Scotland, 25 December 1840. [RSC.I.206]

MACDONALD, WILLIAM, a student at the Scots College in Valladolid, Spain, 1794. [RSC.I.211]

MACDONEL, ALEXANDER, born in March 1698, son of Donald MacDonel and Catharine MacLean, in the Diocese of Galloway, a student at the Scots College in Rome, 1717. [RSC.I.129]

MACDONELL, ALEXANDER, {'Pickle the Spy'}, of Glengarry, a Jacobite banished in 1748, in Rome 1750. [Stuart Papers at Windsor, 193]

MACDONELL, ALEXANDER, born 1740, son of Aeneas MacDonell and Catherine MacLeod in the diocese of the Isles, a student at the Scots College in Rome, 1759, died in America. [RSC.I.139]

MACDONELL, ALEXANDER, a student at the Scots College in Valladolid, Spain, 1778, ordained there on 20 August 1787, a missionary in Scotland and chaplain to the Glengarry Fencibles, emigrated to Canada, a Bishop there by 1825, died in Dumfries, Scotland, on 4 January 1840. [RSC.I.208]

MACDONELL, ALLAN, a student at the Scots College in Valladolid, Spain, 1778, ordained as a missionary in November 1787, died in Edinburgh during February 1809. [RSC.I.208]

MACDONNELL, ANTHONY MARIA, only surviving son of Alexander MacDonnell a Lieutenant General in the service of the King of Portugal, was granted the lands of Glengarry on 3 February 1818. [RGS.157.14.26]

SCOTS IN SOUTHERN EUROPE, 1600-1900

MACDONELL, AUGUSTINE, a student at the Scots College in Rome 1786, possibly at Valladolid, Spain, 1788, died there. [RSC.I.145/210]

MACDONELL, JOHN, born in the diocese of the Isles, a student at
the Scots College in Rome, 1740. [RSC.I.134]

MACDONELL, JOHN, born 1734 in the diocese of Ross, a student at
the Scots College in Rome, 1751. [RSC.I.136]

MACDONELL, JOHN, son of Aeneas MacDonell in the Diocese of the Isles, a student at the Scots College in Rome 1782.[RSC.I.145]

MACDONELL, KATHARINE, daughter of Alexander MacDonell of
the cavalry in Portugal, and niece of Colonel John MacDonell of the 76th Regiment, died in Perth on 16 May 1782. [SM.44.280]

MACDOUGAL, BARBARA, second daughter of Sir Henry Hay MacDougall of Makerstoun, died in Madeira on 9 July 1810. [SM.72.718][ARM]

MACDOUGAL, JOHN, a student at the Scots College in Valladolid,
Spain, 1780, a missionary who died on St Vincent's . [RSC.I.208]

MACDOUGALL, HELEN LOUISA, eldest daughter of Sir Henry
Hay MacDougall of Makerstoun, baronet, died in Madeira on 27 October 1810. [SM.73.77]

SCOTS IN SOUTHERN EUROPE, 1600-1900

MACDOUGALL, JOHN SAMSON, a merchant in Seville, 1893.
[NRS.CS46.1893.2.65]

MCDOWALL, ROLAND JAMES, of Logan, died in Florence, 28 December 1861, inventory, 1862, Comm. Edinburgh. [NRS]

MACEACHEN, RONALD, (Reginaldus Makichen), son of Ronald MacEachen and Merois MacDonald, born in the Diocese of the Isles 6 December 1756, a student at the Scots College in Rome, 1772. [RSC.I.143]

MCEACHREN, ANGUS, a student at the Scots College at Valladolid, Spain, 1777, Bishop of the Isles, 1821. [RSC.I.207]

MCEWAN, ARCHIBALD JAMES MAITLAND, born 1857, son of Reverend Archibald McEwan in Dumfries, married Caroline Wilkinson, in the Anglican Church in Madeira on 19 July 1880. [ARM]

MACFARLANE, ALEXANDRINA JOHNSTONE, born 1833, died 31 December 1910, buried in the British Cemetery in Funchal, Madeira. [ARM]

MACFARLANE, CHRISTINE JOHNSTONE, died in Madeira 7 May 1809. [ARM]

MCFARLANE, GEORGE, from Mauchline, Ayrshire, a volunteer under Garibaldi, in Italy 1860. [SHR.57.176]

MACFARLANE, MARGARET FLETCHER, born 1830, died and was buried in the British Cemetery, Funchal, Madeira, on 24 August 1919. [ARM]

MCFARLANE, Lieutenant Colonel ROBERT, married Maria Gertrude Van Kemper, eldest daughter of Gervais Henry Van

SCOTS IN SOUTHERN EUROPE, 1600-1900

Kemper, Dutch Consul in Tripoli, in Palermo, Sicily, in 1815.
[SM.77.399]

MACFIE, NEIL, born in May 1702, son of Donald MacFie and his wife Marian Wright, in the Diocese of the Isles, a student at the Scots College in Rome, 1717. [RSC.I.129]

MACGHIE, ANDREW, a student at the Scots College in Rome, 1654, a Jesuit missionary in Scotland, 1654. [RSC.I.115]

MACGHILLIS, AENEAS, born October 1745, son of Duncan MacGhillis and Catharina MacEachen in the Diocese of the Isles, a student at the Scots College in Rome, 1765, died 1812. [RSC.I.140]

MACGILL, ANN, eldest daughter of Thomas MacGill in Malta, wife of John Mackenzie, died in Naples on 22 February 1818. [SM.81.395]

MAKGILL, JOHN, a student at the University of Padua, 1677. [RCPE]

MCGILL, THOMAS, born in Port Glasgow during 1774, Knight of the Order of the Redeemer of Greece, Consul to Greece and Bavaria, author, died in Malta on 8 October 1844. [AJ#5054][GrA: 15.11.1844]

MCGILL, WILLIAM, rector of the Scots College in Madrid, 1727-1734. [RSC.I.203]

MACGILLIS, AENEAS, from the diocese of Argyll, a student at the Scots College in Rome, 1730. [RSC.I.132]

MACGILLIVRAY, ANGUS, a student at the Scots College in Valladolid, Spain, 1777, died 21 June 1778. [RSC.I.207]

SCOTS IN SOUTHERN EUROPE, 1600-1900

MACGLASHAN, Captain NEIL, of the 42nd Regiment, aged 22, eldest son of Major MacGlashan of Eastertyre, died in Lisbon on 9 July 1811 after the battle of Fuentes de Honor. [SM.73.716] [Cemiterio dos Inglezes, Lisbon]

MACGREGOR, DUNCAN DRUMMOND, son of Malcolm MacGregor and his wife Fanny Gleek, was born 20 December 1808 and baptised 12 January 1809 in the Anglican Church of Madeira. [ARM]

MACGREGOR, JOHN, son of John MacGregor and Elisabeth Lauson in the Diocese of St Andrews and Edinburgh, a student at the Scots College in Rome, 1701. [RSC.I.125]

MACGREGOR, Sir WILLIAM, born 1698, son of Sir Alexander MacGregor of Balhaldies, a Jacobite in Italy, 1740s. [Memorials of John Murray, Edinburgh, 1898]

MCGUCHIN, CHARLES A., Lieutenant of the 1st Battalion of the 38th Regiment of Foot, died in battle at San Sebastian, Spain, in 1813. [SM.75.799]

MCHATTIE, JOHN, a student at the Scots College in Valladolid, Spain, 1771, died in April 1774. [RSC.I.205]

MCINTOSH, ALEXANDER, judge advocate in Gibraltar, was admitted as a burgess and guilds-brother of Glasgow on 20 September 1728. [GBR]

MACINTOSH, CHARLES, a merchant in Gibraltar, a deed, 1766, [NRS.RD2.218.198]; a sasine 1776. [NRS.RS38.XIII.413]

MCINTOSH, CHARLES, born 25 November 1848, son of Angus McIntosh and his wife Ann McKenzie, a student at Valladollid, Spain, died there on 22 August 1866. [Braemar gravestone]

SCOTS IN SOUTHERN EUROPE, 1600-1900

MACKINTOSH, Dr DUNCAN, in the Canary Islands, son of John Mackintosh of Culclachy and Janet, daughter of William Mackintosh of Aberarder, 3 April 1759. [NRS.Lyon.GI.52]

MACKINTOSH, D., a merchant in Leghorn, Italy, son of Alexander Mackintosh [1763-1794], and his wife Ann McKillican [1767-1851]. [Croy, Inverness-shire, MI]

MACINTOSH, DUNCAN, born during 1779, son of Andrew MacIntosh a merchant in Forres, Morayshire, a surgeon who died in Spain on 10 May 1813. [SM.75.478]

MACINTOSH, LACHLAN, born 12 July 1704, son of Duncan MacIntosh and his wife Helen Gordon in the Diocese of Moray, a student at the Scots College in Rome, 1721. [RSC.I.130]

MACINTOSH, LACHLAN, a merchant in Gibraltar later in London, 1776. [NRS.RS38.XII.410]

MACINTOSH, LACHLAN, born 1752, a student at the Scots College in Valladolid, Spain, 1771, a missionary in Glengairn, died 3 March 1846. [RSC.I.205]

MCINTYRE, Captain JAMES, of the 13th Royal Veteran Battalion, was severely wounded at the battles of Albuera and Almeida when Captain of the 71st Regiment of Foot, died in Lisbon, Portugal, on 27 January 1814. [SM.76.396]

MACKAY, AENEAS, born 1868, died in Madeira 22 August 1927. [ARM]

MCKELLAR, Colonel PATRICK, Chief Engineer in Minorca, died there 22 October 1778. [SM.40.686]

SCOTS IN SOUTHERN EUROPE, 1600-1900

MACKENZIE, Major General JOHN RANDOLL, of Suddie, Lieutenant Colonel of the 78th Regiment of Foot, Member of Parliament for Sutherland, died at the Battle of Talavera de la Reyna on 26 July 1809. [SM.71.717]

MCKINLAY, FLORA, born 1827, from the Isle of Lewis, wife of Richard C. Smith, died 10 November 1854, buried in the British Cemetery, Funchal, Madeira. [ARM]

MCINTYRE, AENEAS, a student at the Scots College in Rome 1792. [RSC.I.146]

MCINTYRE, ALISON NAISMITH, wife of James Fortune, died in Malta on 17 January 1898. [S#17037]

MCIVER, HENRY RONALD HISLOP, a volunteer under Garibaldi
in 1860, formerly a soldier in the service of the East India
Company, a sergeant and later a lieutenant in the Legion de
Flotte, finally he fought for the Confederate States and died at
Gettysburg. [SHR.57.172]

MCKAIL, JOHN, born 1810 in Ayrshire, son of Hugh McKail a farmer, minister of the Scots Church in Malta and chaplain to the Black Watch there 1843-1846. [F.7.556]

MCKELLAR, LINDSAY, in Minorca, a deed, 4 July 1792. [NRS.RD3.257.84]; a deed, 6 July 1792. [NRS.RD3.257.84]

MCKELLAR, Colonel PATRICK, of Drumfin, chief engineer in Minorca, a deed of factory, 17 February 1776. [NRS.RD4.219.490]; died there on 22 October 1778. [SM.40.686]

MCKENZIE, FRANCES CATHERINE, daughter of Lord Seaforth,

died in Rome 24 February 1840, inventory, 1848, Comm. Edinburgh. [NRS]

MACKENZIE, FRANCIS JAMES NAPIER, born in Edinburgh on 19 October 1837, Colonel of the Bengal Staff Corps, died in Rome on 19 November 1884. [Protestant Cemetery in Rome, MI]

MCKENZIE, GEORGE, a Jacobite in Urbino, 1718. [JU]

MCKENZIE, JOHN, married Anne MacGill, eldest daughter of Thomas MacGill, Malta, in Valetta on 16 December 1817. [SM.81.294]

MCKENZIE, KENNETH, son of Hector McKenzie and his wife Joan McKenzie, a student at the Scots College in Madrid, 1722. [RSC.I.200]

MACKENZIE, NANCY COPLEY, daughter of Lewis Mackenzie of Tarbet and Scatwell and his wife Nancy, and widow of Thomas Antony Lister, died in Rome on 11 January 1903. [Protestant Cemetery in Rome, MI]

MACKENZIE, RODERICK, of Flowerburn, died in Madeira on 29 November 1848, inventory, 1850, Comm. Edinburgh. [NRS]

MCKENZIE, ROSSLYN JANET, born 1808, daughter of John and Elizabeth McKenzie, died in Florence on 12 November 1838, wife of .... Wedderburn. [Florence MI]

MACKENZIE, ..., son of Deputy Commissary General John Mackenzie, was born in Gibraltar, 1818. [SM.82.294]

MCKINLAY, FLORA, born 1827, from the Isle of Lewis, died 10 November 1854, buried in the British Cemetery in Funchal, Madeira. [ARM]

SCOTS IN SOUTHERN EUROPE, 1600-1900

MACKINLAY, Dr ROBERT, a physician in Rome and Turin, 1760s. [NRS.GD248]

MCKINNON, ALEXANDER, a merchant in Leghorn, Italy, was admitted as a burgess of Banff in 1786. [Banff Burgess Roll]; a merchant in Naples, in Edinburgh by 1800, husband of Mary Emilia daughter of Charles MacKinnon of MacKinnon. [NRS.CC8.6.1090][SGS]

MCKINNON, ALEXANDER, a banker in Naples, married Miss McKinnon of McKinnon, in Edinburgh on 5 October 1792. [SM.53.517]

MACKINTOSH, DUNCAN, a surgeon to the forces, son of Andrew Mackintosh a merchant in Forres, died in Spain on 10 May 1813, aged 34. [SM.75.478]

MACKNIGHT, WILLIAM, MD, born 22 April 1771, son of Reverend Thomas Somerville and his wife Martha Charters in Jedburgh, died in Florence on 26 June 1860. [F.2.128]

MCLACHLAN, JAMES, a student at the Scots College in Rome 1786. [RSC.I.145]

MCLACHLAN, JOHN, born 1692, son of Donald MacLachlan and his wife Beatrix Campbell in the Diocese of Argyll, a student at the Scots College in Rome, 1715. [RSC.I.128]

MCLACHLAN, PETER, a student at the Scots College in Rome 1792. [RSC.I.145]

MCLAURIN, Rev. JAMES BREARCLIFFE,from Edinburgh, died
in Malaga on 3 January 1858, inventory, 1859, Comm. Edinburgh. [NRS]

SCOTS IN SOUTHERN EUROPE, 1600-1900

MCLAURIN, ..., a merchant in Leghorn (Liverno), 1799. [NRS.GD51.2.100.1/2]

MCLEAN, ALLAN, a Lieutenant of the 91st Regiment, son of Lachlan McLean of Bunessain, died at Vittoria, Spain, on 24 November 1813, from wounds received in the Pyrenees on 26 July 1813.[SM.76.157]

MACLEAN, Sir HECTOR, a Jacobite in 1745, died in Rome 1750. [Oliphants of Gask, p.222]

MACLEAN, JOHN, from the Diocese of Argyll, a student at the Scots College in Rome, 1690. [RSC.I.122]

MACLEAN, JOHN HUGH, born 1797, son of Alexander MacLean of Ardgowar, Argyll, and his wife Lady Margaret MacLean, died in Rome on 6 February 1826. [Protestant Cemetery in Rome, MI][SM.97.511]

MACLEAN, KENNETHINA, born Inverness on 20 May 1857, died in Rome on 17 January 1939. [Protestant Cemetery in Rome, MI]

MACLEAN, Lieutenant General, Governor of Lisbon in 1763, Governor of Estramadura in 1773.

MCLELLAN, JAMES, a student at the Scots College in Rome 1792. [RSC.I.145]

MCLEOD, JOHN, Clerk of the Ordnance in Gibraltar, heir to his father Aeneas McLeod, Lieutenant Colonel of the Marines, 11 January 1743. [NRS.S/H]

SCOTS IN SOUTHERN EUROPE, 1600-1900

MACLEOD, WILLIAM, a student at the Scots College in Valladoild, Spain, 1788, later priest in Braemar, died 3 July 1809. [RSC.I.210]

MACLEOD, WILLIAM, born 1791, late First Lieutenant of HMS La Virginie, and fourth son of Donald MacLeod of Geanies, Ross-shire, died in Lisbon on 30 March 1805. [SM.67.327]; letters,. [NLS.GB233.ms19305]

MCMATH, JOHN, land major in Tangiers, was admitted as a burgess of Edinburgh on 10 October 1679, testament, 1695, Commissariat of Edinburgh. [NRS]

MCNAB, ALLAN, a Lieutenant of the 92nd Regiment, died on 14 May 1811 from wound received at Almeida on 5 April 1811. [SM.73.558]

MCNAB, JOHN, son of Duncan McNab and his wife Anne MacLachlan in the Diocese of Dunkeld, a student at the Scots College in Rome 1778. [RSC.I.144]

MCNAIR, PHILIP BARTON, aged 21, second son of James McNair of Greenfield, Glasgow, died in Madeira on 8 January 1813. [SM.75.318][ARM]

MCNEADER, WILLIAM, born 1757, a clerk from Scotland, via London to Cadiz aboard the Agnes in1774. [TNA.T47.9/11]

MACNEAL, HENRY, Captain in Colonel Reid's regiment in Gibraltar, died 1737. [SM.I.141]

MACNEIL, RANALD, a student at the Scots College in Valladolid, Spain, 1780, died in the East Indies. [RSC.I.209]

SCOTS IN SOUTHERN EUROPE, 1600-1900

MCNEILL, JOHN, born in May 1747, son of Hector MacNeill and his wife Catharina Campbell in the diocese of the Isles, a student at the Scots College in Rome, 1765. [RSC.I.140]

MCNICOLL, GRACE, infant daughter of Nicol McNicoll, died in Belmont, Lisbon, Portugal, on 7 July 1884. [S#12790]

MCNIEL, ..., daughter of Roderick McNiell, was born in Florence, Italy, on 18 September 1819. [SM.84.485]

MCNIVEN, ARCHIBALD, born 1793, from Little Mill, Dunbartonshire, died 20 February 1869, buried in the British Cemetery in Funchal, Madeira. An engineer aboard USS Portsmouth [ARM]

MACPHERSON, ANDREW, born 1880, married Elsie Barbara Shaw, born 1885, in the Presbyterian Church in Madeira in 1911. [ARM]

MACPHERSON, DANIEL, from Inverness, married Josepha Hemas of Cadiz, Spain, there on 14 April 1819. [SM.83.583]

MACPHERSON, PAUL, born 1756, a student at the Scots College in Valladolid, Spain, 1777, later in Rome, died 24 November 1846. [RSC.I.207]

MACPHERSON, ..., daughter of John MacPherson, was born in Rome on 7 April 1819. [SM.83.582]

MCPHERON, WILLIAM, British vice consul in Seville, Spain, in 1878, a letter. [NRS.GD164.1566]

MCPHERSON, JAMES, alias Don Diego McPherson, Captain of Spanish Grenadiers, a prisoner at Berwick, 1747. [P.1.246]

SCOTS IN SOUTHERN EUROPE, 1600-1900

MCPHERSON, JAMES, a student at the Scots College in Rome 1786. [RSC.I.145]

MCPHERSON, JAMES, Captain of the 42nd Regiment, died in Lebau, Spain, on 6 November 1809. [SM.72.158]

MCPHERSON, JESS, in Madeira, a letter, 1846. [NRS.GD176.2244]

MCPHERSON, JOHN HYNDMAN, midshipman aboard the frigate <u>Renommee</u>, son of the late Alexander McPherson a merchant in Glasgow, died in Gibraltar on 13 March 1808. [SM.70.477]

MACPHERSON, PAUL, born 7 January 1756, son of Paul MacPherson and his wife Joan Cumming in Morayshire, a student at the Scots College in Rome, 1770, died in Rome 24 November 1846. [RSC.I.142]

MACPHERSON, THOMAS, a student at the Scots College in Rome, 1622, later in Paris, also chaplain to the Douglas Regiment. [RSC.I.106]

MCPHERSON, ..., son of Major McPherson of the 10th Portuguese Cavalry, was born in Portugal in 1815. [SM.85.388]

MCPHERSON-GRANT, JOHN, British attaché in Turin, Italy, in 1830. [NRS.NRAS.771, bundle 117]

MACRA, CHRISTOPHER, born 1764, a student at the Scots College in Valladolid, Spain, 1780, ordained in November 1787, a missionary in Kintail, died 27 September 1842. [RSC.I.209]

MCVICAR, JOHN ARCHIBALD, born 1843, Captain of the 93rd [Sutherland] Highlanders, died in Rome on 21 January 1880. [Protestant Cemetery in Rome, MI][DCA#8276]

SCOTS IN SOUTHERN EUROPE, 1600-1900

MAIN, EDWARD, a merchant in Lisbon, Portugal, 1743, 1746. [NRS.AC9.1525/1619]

MAIN, JOHN, a student at the Scots College in Rome, 1619, later in Wurzburg. [RSC.I.106]

MAIN, JOHN, a merchant in Lisbon, Portugal, was granted the lands of Powhouse in Scotland on 12 February 1731, [NRS.RGS.93.50]; a merchant burgess of Edinburgh in 1736; a merchant in Lisbon, Portugal, in 1743, 1746. [NRS.AC9.1525/1619][SGS]

MAITLAND, ALEXANDER, a Jacobite in Urbino, Italy, 1717, died in September 1717. [JU]

MAITLAND, THOMAS, Governor of Malta, died there of apoplexy, 17 January 1824. [SM.93.383]

MALCOLMSON, SIMON, born 1844, died 1870 in Malta. [Cunningsburgh MI, Shetland Islands]

MALLOCH, JOHN, master of the Darien Company ship the Dolphin, imprisoned in Carthagena and in Seville, Spain, in 1700 accused of piracy. [NRS. GD406.1.4541]

MANSON, ALEXANDER, MD, second son of Alexander Manson of Oakhill, Aberdeenshire, surgeon at the Turkish Hospital in Jaffa, Palestine, died 9 May 1841. [AJ.4886]

MARSHALL, JOHN, from Edinburgh, a student at Padua University, Italy, in 1717. [RCPE]

MARSHALL, JOHN, a merchant in Oporto, Portugal, son of James Marshall a merchant in Auchtermuchty, Fife, a deed, 1769. [NRS.SC20.36.12]

SCOTS IN SOUTHERN EUROPE, 1600-1900

MARTIN, JOHN ECCLES, a merchant in Lisbon, Portugal, died 3 August 1856, inventory, 1856, Comm. Edinburgh. [NRS]

MARTIN, WILLIAM, born 1789, MD, died in Malta on 6 March 1843, husband of Eliza Gilley, born 1795, died in Malta on 31 August 1840. [Dollar MI][SGS]

MARTINA, JOSEPH, born in Turin, Piedmont, Italy, during May 1802, a teacher of Italian in Edinburgh, died 17 January 1837, inventory, 1837, Comm. Edinburgh. [NRS][St Cuthbert's MI. Edinburgh]

MASTERTON, JAMES, second son of Francis Masterton of Parkmill and Gogar, Perthshire, [1716-1795], partner of Arthur Achmuty in firm of Ahmuty, Masterton and Company, merchant in Madeira, from 1787. Husband of Ann Amelia Murdoch, daughter of James Murdoch in Madeira. Partner with James Murdoch, Thomas Yuille in London, Andrew Wardrop and James Denyer both in Madeira, as merchants in firm of Murdoch, Masterton and Company from 1800. He returned to Scotland and settled at Braco, Perthshire, where he died 1 April 1836. [NRS.RD4.258/980; RD4.268/276-7][SHS.XV.465]

MATHISON, GEORGE, born 1756, a student at the Scots College in Valladolid, Spain, 1771, a missionary in Scotland, died 14 January 1828. [RSC.I.205]

MATTHEW, WILLIAM, born 1837, formerly of the 2nd Edinburgh Highland Rifles, a volunteer in Italy under Garibaldi, 1860. [SHR.57.175]

MATTHEWS, N, from Edinburgh, a volunteer in Italy under Garibaldi, 1860. [SHR.57.176/177]

SCOTS IN SOUTHERN EUROPE, 1600-1900

MAULE, JAMES, Earl of Panmure, son of George Maule, a Jacobite at the Battle of Sheriffmuir, fled to France, a Jacobite in Urbino, Italy, in 1717, died in Paris on 6 April 1720. [JU][SP.VII.26]

MAXWELL, FREDERICK, son of the Baron of Herries, a student at the Scots College in Madrid, Spain, 1632, later rector of the Scots College in Madrid from 1656-1659, died 9 May 1659. [RSC.I.195/202]

MAXWELL, JOHN, from Nithsdale, a student at the Scots College in Rome, 1616. [RSC.I.105]

MAXWELL, ROBERT, born 1628, son of James Maxwell and his wife Alice Collins, a student at the Scots College in Madrid, Spain, 1647. [RSC.I.197]

MAXWELL, THOMAS, of the family of Nithsdale, a student at the Scots College in Valladolid, Spain, 1664, later a soldier in Ireland, France and Italy. [RSC.I.198]

MAYNE, EDWARD, from Logie, Perthshire, a merchant in Lisbon, Portugal, who died during March 1743. [NRS.S/H]

MAYNE, EDWARD, in Lisbon, a deed of attorney with Alexander Jaffrey, 21 September 1807. [NRS.RD2.301.664]

MAYNE, THOMAS, a merchant in Lisbon, Portugal, died there on 14 January 1795. [SM.57.206]

MAYNE, Lieutenant, of HMS Polyphemus, married Miss E. Stuart, daughter of ..... Stuart a master attendant in Gibraltar, there in November 1805. [SM.67.966]

MEASON, GILBERT LAING, died 1832. [Protestant Cemetery in Rome, MI]

SCOTS IN SOUTHERN EUROPE, 1600-1900

MELDRUM, or BAILLIE, WILLIAM, a student at the Scots College in Rome, 1657, later a missionary in Scotland and England. [RSC.I.116]

MELVILLE, DAVID, aged 21, a Lieutenant of the Royal Engineers, third son of John Melville of Dysart, was killed at Badajos on 12 May 1811. [SM.73.558]

MELZI, Count, from Rome, was admitted as a burgess of Glasgow on 18 July 1787. [GBR]

MENZIES, GEORGE, a Jacobite in Urbino, Italy, in 1717. [JU]

MENZIES, GILBERT, from Aberdeen, a student at the Scots College in Rome, 1657. [RSC.I.116]

MENZIES, JOHN, born in the parish of St Machar's, Aberdeen, son of Thomas Menzies of Balgownie and his wife Margaret Gordon of Grandholm, a student at the Scots College in Madrid, Spain, 1647. [RSC.I.197]

MENZIES, JOHN, a student at Padua University, Italy, 1659. [RCPE]

METHVEN, JAMES, a gas engineer, died in Oporto, Portugal, on 5 May 1857. [PJD.489]

MIDDLETON, GILBERT, a student at the Scots College in Rome, 1636. [RSC.I.110]

MILES, ..., a factor in Madeira, 1704. [NRS.AC9.88]

MILL, ANDREW, a student at the Scots College in Rome, 1640. [RSC.I.111]

SCOTS IN SOUTHERN EUROPE, 1600-1900

MILLER, Dr ALEXANDER, born 1809, from Ayrshire, died 17 March 1854, buried in the British Cemetery in Funchal, Madeira. [ARM]

MILLER, ANDREW, born 1819, from Glasgow, died 29 May 1846, buried in the British Cemetery in Funchal, Madeira. [ARM]

MILLAR, ANNIE STEVENSON, born 10 July 1872 in Glasgow, died in Rome on 6 February 1920. [Protestant Cemetery in Rome, MI]

MILLER, DONALD, of the merchant firm Henderson Brothers in Leghorn, [Livorno], Italy, 1859. [SHR.57.168]

MILLER, FLORENCE or FRANCES A., born in Glasgow on 16 January 1851, died in Rome on 12 November 1859. [Protestant Cemetery in Rome, MI]

MILLER, MARY ANNE ELIZABETH, widow of Reverend George Lewis, born in Edinburgh on 26 July 1814, died in Rome on 22 December 1895. [Protestant Cemetery in Rome, MI]

MILLIGAN, WILLIAM, from Kirkbean, Charleston, South Carolina, died 1819 in Madeira. [NRS.CS46.1834.150]

MILLIKEN, JAMES, jr., died in Venice, Italy, on 9 April 1763. [SM.25.301]

MILNE, HENRY, from Aberdeen, an Ensign of the 102nd Regiment of Foot, died in Portugal, 1796. [Anglican Church Records, Lisbon]

MILNE, HENRY, a medical student from Edinburgh, died in Lisbon, Portugal, on 13 March 1789. [SM.51.205]

SCOTS IN SOUTHERN EUROPE, 1600-1900

MINTO, ANDREW, born 1786, son of Alexander Minto a farmer in Kinnore, Huntly, Aberdeenshire, a merchant in Leghorn, [Livorno], Italy, for 30 years, died there on 19 January 1838. [AJ.4717]

MITCHELL, Dr ANDREW, son of the late Sir Andrew Mitchell of Wellshore, baronet, died in Rome in 1780. 'He died of an epidemic fever he had contracted by attending the hospitals'. [SM.42.673]

MITCHELL, DUNCAN FORBES, Lieutenant of <u>HMS Victory</u>, died in Naples, Italy, in 1796. [SM.58.289]

MITCHELL, JOHN, a glass merchant from Italy who settled in Edinburgh around 1768, residing in West Bow, Edinburgh, in 1794. [ECA.SL115.1.1]

MITCHELL, THOMAS, a Lieutenant of the Rifle Brigade, eldest son of the late Mr Mitchell, collector of Shore-dues and harbour-master of Grangemouth, married Mary Blunt, eldest daughter of Lieutenant General Blunt, in Lisbon, Portugal, in 1818. [SM.82.587]

MITCHELL, WILLIAM, a student at the Scots College in Rome, 1677. [RSC.I.119]

MITCHELL, ..., from Glasgow, a volunteer under Garibaldi, killed at Capua, Italy, in 1860. [SHR.57.177]

MITCHELSON, JAMES, a merchant, died in Lisbon, Portugal, during April 1760. [SM.22.334]

MOFFAT, WILLIAM, of Prinlaws, paymaster of the 79th Regiment, died in a Portuguese village on 19 October 1810 when bound for
Lisbon, Portugal. [SM.72.959]

SCOTS IN SOUTHERN EUROPE, 1600-1900

MOIR, ADAM, an architect in Gibraltar, power of attorney, 1827. [NRS.SC67.49.14.266]

MOIR, JACOB, a painter, died in Rome on 1 September 1793. [SM.55.619]

MOIR, JOSEPH, a Lieutenant of the Royal Sicilian Corps, 1799. [NRS.GD155.1279]

MONCRIEFF, FRANCIS, youngest son of Dr Moncrieff in Bristol, died in Pisa, Italy, in 1794. [SM.56.588]

MONRO, ALEXANDER, a merchant in Lisbon, Portugal, testament, 13 August 1741, Commissariat of Edinburgh. [NRS]

MONRO, Dr GEORGE, late HM physician in Minorca, Balearic Islands, died in Edinburgh on 24 February 1793. [SM.55.102]; deeds, 12 March 1793; 10 May 1793. [NRS.RD4.253.482/913]

MONRO, JOHN, a student at Padua University, Italy, 1700. [RCPE]

MONRO, Miss MARY, daughter of the late John Monro a merchant in Edinburgh, married Richard Grey a merchant in Lisbon, Portugal, there in 1813. [SM.75.473]

MONRO, ROBERT, from Ross-shire, a student at the Scots College in Rome, 1668. [RSC.I.1668]

MONTEITH, JOHN, a volunteer under Garibaldi, in Italy 1860. [SHR.57.176]

MONTGOMERY, ARCHIBALD, in Gibraltar, a letter, 1750. [NRS.GD16.34.367]

SCOTS IN SOUTHERN EUROPE, 1600-1900

MONTGOMERY, JOHN, a merchant in Lisbon, Portugal, died there on 6 November 1786. [SM.48.571]

MONTGOMERY, ..., son of Lady Montgomery, was born in Palermo, Italy, on 28 September 1812. [SM.74.966

MONTGOMERY, Lord, only son of the Earl of Eglinton, died in Alicante, Spain, on 4 January 1814. [SM.76.237]

MONTEITH, WILLIAM, a student at the Scots College in Rome, 1636, a Jesuit missionary in Scotland, died in England. [RSC.I.110]

MONTOUARD, JOSEPH, born in Italy around 1831, a street musician in Edinburgh by 1851. [Census]

MONYPENNY, FRANCIS, Lieutenant of the 68th Regiment of Foot, died in Gibraltar on 22 August 1791. [SM.53.515]

MOONEY, Mrs MARGARET, born in Gibraltar around 1797, wife of a porter in Edinburgh by 1851. [Census]

MORAY, JAMES, in Rome, Italy, a letter, 1822. [PKA.PE16.bundle 336]

MORE, ALEXANDER, born 1667, from the Diocese of Orkney, a student at the Scots College in Rome, 1686. [RSC.I.121]

MORE, HENRY, from Aberdeen, a student at the Scots College in Rome, 1633, later joined the Order of St Benedict in Germany. [RSC.I.110]

MORE, SARAH, born in Portugal around 1812, a resident of Edinburgh by 1851. [Census]

SCOTS IN SOUTHERN EUROPE, 1600-1900

MORISON, COLIN, born 1735, died in Rome, Italy, in June 1809. [SM.71.878]

MORRISON, JAMES, born 1849, son of James Morrison, a manufacturer, [1800-1867], and his wife Margaret Paton, [1810-1878], in Alva, Clackmannanshire, died 19 December 1868, buried in the British Cemetery in Funchal, Madeira. [ARM][Alva MI, Clackmannanshire]

MORRISON, JAMES, in Tharsis, Huelva, Spain, a deed, 1878. [NRS.SC49.78.155]

MORTIMER, GEORGE, from Aberdeen, a student at the Scots College in Rome, 1608. [RSC.I.102]

MORTIMER, ROBERT, from Aberdeen, a student at the Scots College in Rome, 1613, later a Jesuit missionary in Scotland. [RSC.I.104]

MORTON, the EARL of, died in Sicily on 28 September 1774. [SM.36.559]

MORTON, P., in Milan, Italy, a letter, 1636. [NRS.GD406.1.9591]

MOUAT, JAMES, born 1756, died 15 July 1819 on Madeira. [ARM]

MOULTRIE, THOMAS, Captain of the 7th Royal Fusiliers, died at Elvas on 10 June 1811 from wounds received at the Battle of Albuera, Spain. [SM.73.637]

MOWBRAY, ROBERT C., son of William Mowbray a merchant in Leith, died in Rome, Italy, on 2 March 1823. [SM.86.648]

SCOTS IN SOUTHERN EUROPE, 1600-1900

MUDIE, WILLIAM, settled in Alicante, Spain, a burgess of Montrose in 1798. [SGS]

MUIR, CATHERINE, born 1811, of Muir Park, Port Glasgow, died in Madeira on 10 April 1834. [ARM]

MUIR, JOHN, a merchant in Madeira, died 1832. [ARM]

MUIR, MATTHEW E., a merchant in Oporto, Portugal, and Jane McL. Gow, a marriage contract, 1886. [NRS.RD5.2068/375/108]

MUIR, THOMAS, born 1808, died on Madeira, 17 June 1829. [ARM]

MUIRHEAD, alias GROSSET, JAMES, of Breadisholm, a merchant in Lisbon, Portugal, a sasine, 29 September 1766. [NRS.RS18.15.224]

MUNRO, Sir ALEXANDER, a Customs Commissioner, and late Consul General in Spain, married Miss Johnstone of Tavistock Street, Bedford Square, London, only daughter of the late Andrew Johnstone, at Ripon Minster on 17 July 1791. [SM.53.360]

MUNRO, DONALD, of Lemlair, Ross-shire, born 1814, died in Rome, Italy, on 11 March 1840. [Protestant Cemetery in Rome, MI]

MUNRO, HUGH, born10 August 1782, son of Reverend Alexander Munro minister at Edderton, Easter Ross, and his wife Margaret Cooper, a merchant in Lisbon, Portugal. [F.7.54]

MUNRO, JOHN, of HMS Cambrian, eldest son of George Munro in Glasgow, did in Malta on 17 June 1821. [S.5.246]

SCOTS IN SOUTHERN EUROPE, 1600-1900

MURDOCH, JAMES, a merchant in Quinta do Val, Funchal, Madeira, around 1754. [ARM][OW.36]; one of the oldest British merchants resident in Madeira, died on 11 May 1806. [SM.67.565]

MURDOCH, JOHN, a wine merchants in Madeira, 1768. [OW]

MURDOCH, MICHAEL, son of Alexander Murdoch the procurator fiscal of Ayrshire, died in Malta on 8 January 1848. [SG#1686]

MURDOCH, JAMES and JOHN, wine merchants in Madeira, 1768. In 1786 James Murdoch founded the firm of Murdoch, Fearns and Company, later known as Murdoch and Shortridge. [ARM][OW.136]

MURDOCH, THOMAS, settled in Madeira in 1776, later a partner in Newton, Gordon and Murdoch merchants in Madeira. [ARM]

MURDOCH, WILLIAM, born in Aberdeen, a merchant in Madeira, died there on 27 June 1757. [AJ#502][SM.19.438][OW]

MURDOCH, YUILLE, and WARDROP, wine merchants in Madeira in 1807. [OW.137]

MURRAY, CHARLES, late of Madeira, 1771, reference in will of David Murray in Georgia, son of John Murray of Philiphaugh. Probate South Carolina, 1770.

MURRAY, CHARLES, at Quinta do Belo Monte, Madeira, in1780s; aged 74, son of the late John Murray of
Philiphaugh, and for many years HM Consul in Madeira, residing at Bello Monte, Funchal, Madeira, died in Lisbon, Portugal, in March 1808. [SM.70.398][ARM][OW.36]

SCOTS IN SOUTHERN EUROPE, 1600-1900

MURRAY, JAMES, a secretary, a Jacobite in Urbino, Italy, 1718. [JU]

MURRAY JOHN, of Murraythwaite, a planter in Charleston, South Carolina, trading with Scott, Pringle and Cheap in Madeira in 1757. [NRS.GD219.290]

MURRAY, W. H., a Lieutenant of the 1st Regiment of Foot, drowned in the River Tagus, Portugal, in August 1811. [SM.73.719]

MURRAY, Mrs, widow of Charles Murray, British Consul General in Madeira, and daughter of the late Robert Scott of Crailing, Roxburghshire, died in Edinburgh on 1 December 1806. [SM.69.78]

MURRAY, DAVID, only son of Charles Murray of Stanhope, died in Leghorn, [Livorno], Italy, on 8 October 1770. [SM.32.575]

MURRAY, E. H. P., eldest son of Lieutenant Colonel Murray, died in Naples, Italy, on 10 July 1795. [SM.57.546]

MURRAY, JAMES, a student at the Scots College in Rome, Italy, 1616. [RSC.I.105]

MURRAY, JOHN, of Murraythwaite, a Scottish planter in Charleston, South Carolina, trading with Scott, Pringle and Cheap in Madeira, 1757. [NRS.GD219.290]

MURRAY, JOHN, H.M. Ambassador to the Ottoman Porte, died in Venice, Italy, on 9 August 1775. [SM.37.462]

SCOTS IN SOUTHERN EUROPE, 1600-1900

MURRAY, JOHN, in Barcelona, Spain, in 1795. [NRS.GD219.324]

MURRAY, JOHN, MD, FRCS (Edinburgh), from Aberdeenshire, a member of the Army Medical Department in Malta, Italy, and Sicily, 1804-1813. [NRS.GD1.530.1]

MURRAY, Captain ROBERT, in Gibraltar, husband of Janet Murray, a deed of factory, 1750. [NRS.RD4.176/2.429]

MURRAY, SUSANNA, granted a pass to travel to Portugal, 9 April 1705. [TNA.SP44.390.419]

MURRAY, General THOMAS, died in Malta on 24 April 1816. [SM.78.558]

MURRAY, Miss ..... only daughter of James Murray of Broughton, died in Rome, 1777. [SM.39.279]

MUTER, JAMES, Lieutenant Colonel of the Buffs, eldest son of William Muter of Annfield, died at the Battle of Talavera de la Reyna, Spain, on 28 July 1809. [SM.71.717]

MUTTER, JOHN, from Richmond, Virginia, died in Naples, Italy, on 20 January 1819. [SM.83.286][S.111.19]

NAIRNE, DAVID, a secretary, a Jacobite in Urbino, Italy, 1717. [JU]

NEILL, GILBERT, to Leghorn (Livorno), Italy, a letter 26 April 1664. [NRS.GD172.2459]

NEWTON, ANDREW, a partner in the merchant firm Newton and Gordon in Funchal, Madeira, moved to Virginia and imported the firm's Madeira wine. [OW]

SCOTS IN SOUTHERN EUROPE, 1600-1900

NEWTON, FRANCIS, baptised in 1713, son of Reverend Newton in Earlston, Berwickshire, a Jacobite in 1745, moved to London and later to Madeira; a merchant in Funchal by 1754, he died in London after 1809, his elder brother Andrew Newton in Norfolk, Virginia, acted as his agent there. Francis employed his nephew, David Young, as a clerk in Madeira. [ARM][OW]

NEWTON, THOMAS, son of Reverend Newton in Earlston, Berwickshire, a Jacobite in 1745, a merchant in London, then in New York, finally in Madeira, died in New York between 1766 and 1769. [see Thomas Newton's letter book, Newton and Gordon's ledger 1764-1774, in the Madeira Company Archives, Funchal] The firm of Newton and Gordon was located at 154 Rua dos Ferreiros, Funchal, Madeira. [OW]

NEWTON, GORDON and JOHNSTON, merchants in Madeira, a decreet, 1781. [NRS.CS16.1.183]

NEWTON, GORDON, MURDOCH, and SCOTT, wine merchants in Madeira in 1807. [OW.137]

NICHOL, J., possibly from Glasgow, a volunteer under Garibaldi, in Italy in 1860. [SHR.57.176]

NICOL, JAMES, born 1633, from the Diocese of Moray, a student at the Scots College in Rome, 1677, died in Paris on 2 October 1696. [RSC.I.119]

NISBET, GEORGE, a student at Padua University, Italy, in 1645. [RCPE]

NISBET, HENRY, a student at the Scots College in Rome, 1632. [RSC.I.109]

NISBET, HENRY, a student at Padua University, in Italy, in 1640s. [RCPE]

SCOTS IN SOUTHERN EUROPE, 1600-1900

NITHSDALE, Earl of, a Jacobite in Urbino, Italy, in 1717; died in Rome on 20 March 1744. [JU][SM.6.198]

NITHSDALE, the Countess Dowager, died in Rome, 1749. [SM.11.253]

NOBLE, CHARLES H., in Oporto, Portugal, and Agnes Graham, a marriage contract, 1838. [NRS.RD972.114.22]

NOBLE, CHARLES, born 1855, died in Italy in 1874, buried in the English Cemetery in Naples, Italy. [Port Glasgow MI]

NORTON, CAROLINE ELIZABETH CONYERS, born in Scotland 1798, died in Madeira 22 July 1875, [ARM]; an inventory, 1873. [NRS.SC70.180.471]

ODIE, JOHN IGNATIUS, born 1699, a student at the Scots College in Madrid, 1715, later in Arragon, Spain. [RSC.I.199]

OGILVIE, ALEXANDER, Lord Banff, commander of the man o'war Tilbury, died in Lisbon, Portugal, in 1746. [SM.8.598]

OGILVIE, EMILY, grand-daughter of William Ogilvie of Ardglass Castle, married Count Gurge de Very, in Genoa, Italy, in 1817. [SM.81.94]

OGILVY, Dr GEORGE, aged 32, physician to H.M. Forces, died in Portugal on 4 December 1809. [SM.72.158]

OGILVY, HENRY, educated at the Scots College in Paris, and at the Scots College in Valladolid, Spain, 1773. [RSC.I.205]

OGILVIE, JAMES, a merchant, died on Minorca, Spain, on 8 July 1767. [SM.29.390]

SCOTS IN SOUTHERN EUROPE, 1600-1900

OGILVY, JAMES WEDDERBURN, of Rannagulzion, Lieutenant Colonel of the 25th Regiment, born 4 August 1820, died in Rome on 28 January 1893. [Protestant Cemetery in Rome, MI]

OLIVER, WILLIAM, formerly a merchant in Tarragona, Spain, now in Annan, sasines, 1830/1834. [NRS.B2/2.5.54-58-11]

ONELL, LUKE, a fireworks maker from Italy who settled in Edinburgh during 1784. [ECA.SL115.1.1]

PALMER, JOSEPH, born in Italy around 1805, a hawker of pearl buttons in Edinburgh by 1851. [Census]

PANTON, THOMAS, in Leghorn, [Livorno], Italy, a deed, 1 November 1790. [NRS.RD4.248.1025]

PAPLAY, JAMES, born 1668, from the Diocese of St Andrews, a student at the Scots College in Rome, 1695. [RSC.I.123]

PARK, JAMES HOPE, born in Langholm, Dumfries-shire, on 11 September 1826, died in Rome on 6 March 1891. [Protestant Cemetery in Rome, MI]

PASLEY, JAMES, only son of Robert Pasley of Mount Annan, died in Lisbon, Portugal, on 18 January 1790. [SM.52.102]

PATERSON, ALEXANDER, born 1686, son of William Paterson and his wife 'Maisdra' Stuart in the Diocese of Banff, a student at the Scots College in Rome, 1709, died in Huntly, Aberdeenshire, 16 February 1747. [RSC.I.126]

PATERSON, ALEXANDER, a Lieutenant of the 13th Regiment, died in Gibraltar on 23 October 1804. [SM.67.74]

SCOTS IN SOUTHERN EUROPE, 1600-1900

PATERSON, A. B., born around 1842, a student at Queen's University, Belfast, a volunteer with Garibaldi, fought at the Battle of Milazzo, Italy, later a 1st Lieutenant. [SHR.57.169]

PATERSON, CHARLES, Colonel of the 78th Regiment, fourth son of George Paterson of Castle Huntly, Aberdeenshire, died in Vittoria, Spain on 18 August 1813, inventory, 1838, Comm. Edinburgh. [NRS][SM.75.799]

PATERSON, GEORGE, from Edinburgh, a volunteer under Garibaldi, 1860. [SHR.57.177]

PATERSON, JAMES, in the service of the King of Sardinia, 1716. Brother of the late Sir Hugh Paterson of Bannockburn. [NRS.E616.27.39]; General James Paterson in Sardinia, will, 30 July 1765. [NRS.RD4.198/2.702]

PATERSON, JANE NICOL, born 1844, daughter of Robert Paterson in Glasgow, died 14 March 1862, buried in the British Cemetery, Funchal, Madeira. [ARM]

PATERSON, JOHN, a student at the Scots College in Madrid, Spain, 1632. [RSC.I.195]

PATERSON, JOHN, a secretary, a Jacobite in Urbino, Italy, 1717. [JU]

PATERSON, THOMAS B., son of the late Reverend Robertson minister at Biggar, Lanarkshire, died at Deal, England, on his return from Spain in 1809. [SM.71.880]

PATERSON, WILLIAM, born 1822, from Glasgow, died 12 February 1851, buried in the British Cemetery, Funchal, Madeira. [ARM]

SCOTS IN SOUTHERN EUROPE, 1600-1900

PEARSON, P., possibly from Glasgow, a volunteer in Italy under Garibaldi, 1860. [SHR.57.176]

PEARSON, THOMAS, a student at the Scots College in Rome, 1650. [RSC.I.114]

PENDRICK, ALEXANDER, from Aberdeen, a student at the Scots College in Rome, 1608. [RSC.I.102]

PENMAN, JAMES, late Chief Surgeon of the garrison at Gibraltar, died at Inveresk, Scotland, on 3 March 1745. [SM.7.98]

"PERES", ROBERT, a Scot in Funchal, Madeira, in 1595/ [BRM.2]

PERYNA, MANUEL PERES, in Madeira, 1704. [NRS.AC9.88]

PETRIE, JAMES, from Dunkeld, Perthshire, a student at the Scots College in Rome, 1689. [RSC.I.121]

PHILIP, ROBERT, from Glasgow, a student at the Scots College in Rome, 1602. [RSC.I.101]

PIEROLLI, JOHN, a stucco image maker from Italy who settled in Edinburgh in 1793. [ECA.SL115.1.1]

PINKERTON, ROBERT, master of the Darien Company ship the Endeavour, imprisoned in Carthagena and in Seville, Spain, in 1700 accused of piracy. [NRS.GD224.171.16; GD406.1.4541]

PISCATORE, LEONARDO, Professor of Music in Edinburgh, husband of Susanna Arnauld, a sasine, 1760. [NRS.RS27.156.154]

PLENDERLEATH, Dr JOHN, an army physician, a Member of the Royal College of Physicians in London, third son of Major

SCOTS IN SOUTHERN EUROPE, 1600-1900

Plenderleath, Seymour Street, Edinburgh, died in Coimbra, Portugal, on 18 June 1811. [SM.73.637]

PORTER, JOSEPH, born 1804 in Italy, buried in Dundee Howff on 12 December 1828. [DCA.burial register]

PORTEOUS, WALTER, Commissary General, died in Gibraltar on 29 April 1817. [SM.79.584]

POSSO, PETER, mate aboard the St Antonio of Leghorn, [Livorno], Italy, in 1712. [NRS.AC9.428]

PRESTON, Sir JOHN, a Jacobite in Urbino, Italy, 1717. [JU]

PRINGLE, Mrs CHARLOTTE, spouse to Thomas Mayne a merchant in Lisbon, Portugal, died there on 20 August 1781. [SM.43.503]

PRINGLE, JEAN, wife of Lieutenant Colonel Pringle, commanding engineer in Gibraltar, and daughter of the late Colonel Balneavis of Kirkland, died in Gibraltar on 18 January 1788. [SM.50.206]

PRINGLE, JOHN, from the Diocese of St Andrews, a student at the Scots College in Rome, 1689. [RSC.I.121]

PRINGLE, JOHN, the younger of Crichton, eldest son of Mark Pringle of Crichton, British Consul in St Lucar, Spain, married .... Rutherford, daughter of Robert Rutherford of Fernylees, on 23 April 1752. [SM.14.213]

PRINGLE, JOHN, a merchant in Madeira, second son of the late John Pringle of Haining, was granted the lands of Haining on 10 December 1754. [NRS.RGS.103.62]

SCOTS IN SOUTHERN EUROPE, 1600-1900

PRINGLE, JOSEPH, in Madeira, a letter, 1804.
[NRS.GD51.2.202]; British Consul in Madeira from 1802-1808.

PRINGLE, MARK, in San Lucar, Spain, a letter, 1734.
[NRS.GD18.5403]; son of Andrew Pringle of Clifton, British
consul in Seville, a sasine, 1738. [NRS.RH8.1170]

PRINGLE, Mrs VIOLANTE, wife of Andrew Pringle, an
advocate, and daughter of Mark Pringle of Crichton, British
Consul in St Lucar, Spain, died in Edinburgh of smallpox on 9
December 1753. [SM.15.581]

PURVES, MARGARET, widow of James Brown of Anstruther,
Fife, died in Mina, St Domingo, Portugal, on 28 November 1901.
[East Fife Record]

PURVES, WILLIAM, in Madeira, 1789, with links to Hume of
Polwarth in Scotland. [NRS.GD158.2540]

QUIN, JANE, born 1826 in Corfu, Greece, a millworker in
Scouringburn, Dundee, buried 13 October 1852 in Howff,
Dundee. [DCA.burial register]

RAIT, WILLIAM, in Rome and Venice, Italy, in 1742.
[NRS.GD68.1.308]

RAITT, Captain, of the 42nd [Royal Highlanders] Regiment,
married Miss Walker of Corphin, eldest daughter of Alexander
Walker late Captain of the Royal Fusiliers, in Gibraltar on 15
September 1806. [SM.67.886]

RAMAGE, DICK, in Scotston Park, Lisbon, Portugal, an
inventory, 1 January 1817. [NRS.SC41.68.2/59]

SCOTS IN SOUTHERN EUROPE, 1600-1900

RAMSAY, ERNEST IGNATIUS, from the Diocese of Aberdeen, a student at the Scots College in Rome, 1666. [RSC.I.117]

RAMSAY, JAMES, a student at the Scots College in Rome, 1643, later a priest in France. [RSC.I.112]

RAMSAY, JOHN, in Lisbon, Portugal, 1796, a letter. [NRS.NRAS.3955.60.3.70]

RAMSAY, PETER, son of William Ramsay of Barnton, Lothian, died in Lisbon, Portugal, in 1798. [SM.60.292]

RAMSAY, THOMAS, a student at the Scots College in Rome, 1651. [RSC.I.114]

RAMSAY, Professor WILLIAM, born 1806, died in San Remo, Italy, on 12 February 1865, husband of Catherine who died 19 February 1890. [Alyth gravestone, Perthshire]

RANKIN, NICHOLAS, a Scot aboard the Scots ship, the St James, before the Inquisition in the Canaries, 1591. ['The Inquisition in the Canaries', RHS, London, 1912, p.54]

RATTRAY, WILLIAM, a student at the Scots College in Valladolid, Spain, 1785, ordained in 1796, a missionary in Perth and Dundee, died in Dundee on 1 February 1827. [RSC.I.209]

REDDOCH, NEWTON BURGES, born in Shawlands on 5 April 1845, son of Allan and Janet Reddoch, Laurel Bank, Shawlands, Glasgow, died in Lisbon, Portugal, on 29 March 1874. . [Cemiterio dos Inglezes, Lisbon]

REID, ALEXANDER, a student at the Scots College in Valladolid, Spain, 1771, died in April 1774. [RSC.I.205]

SCOTS IN SOUTHERN EUROPE, 1600-1900

REID, ALEXANDER, born 1851, died 7 December 1881, buried in the British Cemetery in Funchal, Madeira. [ARM]

REID, ALEXANDER, born in Dunfermline, Fife, on 6 September 1820, formerly of Demerara, died in Rome on 29 March 1886. [Protestant Cemetery in Rome, gravestone]

REID, ALFRED EDWARD, born 1866, son of William Reid, a hotelier, married Clara A. Lawson, born 1866, daughter of John Lawson in Glasgow, in the Presbyterian Church in Madeira on 7 July 1890. [ARM]

REID, DAVID, Lieutenant of the Northumberland, youngest son of Andrew Reid a brewer in Canongate, Edinburgh, died in Gibraltar, 1798. [SM.61.72]

REID, EDWARD, born 1630 in London, son of John Reid of Aikenhead and his wife Judith Wekman a Londoner, a student at the Scots College in Madrid, Spain, 1647. [RSC.I.197]

REID, JAMES, a merchant in Gibraltar, 1756. [PRONI.D354-966]

REID, JOHN, born 1629, son of John Reid of Aikenhead and his wife Judith Wekman a Londoner, a student at the Scots College in Madrid, Spain, 1647. [RSC.I.197]

REID, JOHN, born 2 February 1739 in the Diocese of Moray, a student at the Scots College in Rome, 1753, died in Aberdeen during January 1816. [RSC.I.137]

REID, JOHN, born 15 March 1747, son of Alexander Reid and his wife Johanetta Reid in the diocese of Moray, a student at the Scots College in Rome, 1761. [RSC.I.139]

SCOTS IN SOUTHERN EUROPE, 1600-1900

REID, MARGARET, from Glasgow, died and was buried in the British Cemetery, Funchal, Madeira, on 25 March 1858. [ARM]

REID, PETER, son of Alexander Reid and his wife Isabella Blebars in the Diocese of Brechin, a student at the Scots College in Rome, 1702, died in Preshome, 27 November 1726. [RSC.I.125]

REID, WILLIAM, a student at the Scots College in Rome, 1661. [RSC.I.116]

REID, WILLIAM, born 19 June 1712, son of Alexander Reid and Isabella Shand in the Diocese of Aberdeen, a student at the Scots College in Rome, 1733, died in Aberdeen, 26 March 1785. [RSC.I.133]

REID, Sir WILLIAM, born 25 April 1791, son of Reverend James Reid in Kinglassie, Governor of Malta, died January 1859. [SGS]

REID, WILLIAM, a student at the Scots College in Valladolid, Spain, 1780, a missionary in Scotland, died in Dumfries on 27 March 1845. [RSC.I.208]

REMON, Don PEDRO, probably from Cadiz, Spain, was admitted as a burgess and guilds-brother of Ayr on 7 November 1769. [ABR]

RENNIE, ANNA MARIA HONORA, daughter of George Rennie and his wife Jane from Haddington, West Lothian, born in Rome on 25 July 1826, died in Rome on 5 March 1827. [Protestant Cemetery in Rome, gravestone]

RENWICK, Major EDWARD, son of Henry and Jane Renwick, a Lieutenant Colonel in the Service of the Queen of Spain, died in command at Santander, Spain, on 12 January 1836. [St Andrews gravestone, Fife]

RESPIGLIOSI, Prince, of Rome, was admitted as a burgess of Glasgow on 30 July 1788. [GBR]

REZZONICO, Prince, a senator in Rome, was admitted as a burgess of Glasgow on 17 August 1786. [GBR]

RHIND, JOHN, born 1799, son of John Rhind (1759-1826) cashier of the Friendly Insurance Society and his wife Marion Anderson in Edinburgh, (1773-1839), from Edinburgh, died in Madeira on 31 October 1845, and was buried in the British Cemetery, Funchal. [ARM][St Cuthbert's gravestone, Edinburgh]

RICHARDSON, JOHN, in Naples, Italy, a letter, 1821. [PKA.ms101, bundle 85]

RICHARDSON, JOHN, in Leghorn, (Livorno), Italy, died 6 November 1849, inventory, 1854, Comm. Edinburgh. [NRS]

RICHARDSON, ROBERT, in Naples, Italy, and Lisbon, Portugal, letters, 1790s. [PKA.ms101, bundle 45]

RICHBELL, ..., a factor in Madeira, 1704. [NRS.AC9.88]

RICHMOND, THOMAS, from Glasgow, died in Lisbon on 2 January 1852. [FJ#995]

RIGG, CLEMENT, born 1689, son of James Rigg and his wife Elisabeth Wright in the Diocese of Whithorn, a student at the Scots College in Rome, 1709. [RSC.I.126]

RITCHIE, JAMES, born 1816, from 'Balshiemorie', Angus, died 6 February 1878, buried in the British Cemetery in Funchal, Madeira. [ARM]

SCOTS IN SOUTHERN EUROPE, 1600-1900

RITCHIE, ROBERT, HM Consul, died in Venice on 28 December 1790. [SM.52.620]

RITCHIE, WILLIAM, a volunteer under Garibaldi, 1860. [SHR.57.175]

ROACH, GEORGE, in Lisbon, a deed of attorney, 1799. [NRS.RD2.275.808]

ROBB, JAMES, a student at the Scots College in Valladolid, Spain, 1780. [RSC.I.209]

ROBERTSON, ALEXANDER, late a merchant in Aberdeen, died in Nice, France, on 29 April 1841. [AJ#4870]

ROBERTSON, ALEXANDER, born 29 April 1786, son of Reverend Patrick Robertson in Eddleston and his wife Marjory Crawford, a merchant in Florence and Genoa, Italy, died 26 December 1855. [SGS]

ROBERTSON, ALEXANDER, born 1846 in Edinburgh, son of James Robertson and his wife Elizabeth Fairley, minister at San Remo, Liguria, Italy, from 1812 to 1888, minister in Venice, Italy, from 1888. [F.7.555]

ROBERTSON, ALEXANDER, MD, born 1727, surgeon of the 21st Regiment, son of John Robertson, Canongate, Edinburgh, died in Sicily in January 1807. [SM.69.398]

ROBERTSON, ANDREW, a student at the Scots College in Rome, 1614. [RSC.I.104]

ROBERTSON, FRANCIS, a student at the Scots College in Rome, 1653. [RSC.I.115]

SCOTS IN SOUTHERN EUROPE, 1600-1900

ROBERTSON, JAMES, from Dunkeld, Perthshire, a student at the Scots College in Rome, 1687, died there 21 February 1688. [RSC.I.121]

ROBERTSON, MARGARET, born 1826 in Gibraltar, daughter of Charles Robertson a weaver, buried in Dundee on 7 August 1842. [DCA.burial register]

ROBERTSON, WILLIAM, in Mahon, Minorca, Spain, petitioned to import cannons aboard the Elizabeth to defend vessels trading with the Mediterranean seas, 16 March 1777. [JCTP.84.83]

ROBERTSON, WILLIAM, born 2 September 1792 in Eddleston, Peebles-shire, son of Reverend Patrick Robertson and his wife Margaret Crawford, a merchant in Leghorn,[Livorno], Italy, died 11 July 1861. [SGS]

ROBERTSON, ..., son of Dr Henry Robertson, was born in Lisbon , Portugal, on 15 November 1811. [SM.73.876]

ROBINSON, Mrs JANE ELEANOR, wife of Reverend George Robinson of Almorness, died 16 February 1874, aged 58. [Protestant Cemetery in Rome, gravestone]

ROBINSON, MARGARET, born in Edinburgh on 13 January 1788, widow of Archibald McNab of McNab, died in Florence, Italy, on 20 June 1868. [Florence gravestone]

ROLLAND, ROBERT, of Auchmithie, Angus, born 1802, died in Rome on 1 December 1837. [Protestant Cemetery in Rome, gravestone]

ROLLOCK, THOMAS, from Edinburgh, a student at the Scots College in Rome, 1612. [RSC.I.104]

136

SCOTS IN SOUTHERN EUROPE, 1600-1900

ROSE, ALEXANDER, a merchant of Inverness in Leghorn [Livorno], Italy, around 1723. [SIL#202]

ROSE, Major HAMILTON, of the Royal Highlanders, died in Belem, Portugal, on 6 August 1811. [SM.73.798]

ROSE, Reverend HUGH JAMES, Principal of King's College, Aberdeen, died in Florence, Italy, on 22 December 1838. [SG#734]

ROSETTI, JOHN BAPTIST, from Melano, [Milan], Italy, a weather glass and picture maker in Edinburgh 1794. [ECA.SL115.1.1]

ROSIGNOLI, FRANCIS, born in Italy, a fencing master, who settled in Mint Close, Edinburgh, with his sister Teresa, and his mother Rosa, in 1785. [ECA.SL115.1.1]

ROSS, ALEXANDER, of Gibraltar, married Miss Clunes, in Inverness on 19 October 1789. [SM.51.516]

ROSS, ALEXANDER, of Gibraltar, married Helen Inglis, daughter of the late Hugh Inglis a merchant in Inverness, at Kingsmills near Inverness on 21 May 1795. [SM.57.410]

ROSS, GEORGE, son of Alexander Ross of Pitkery and his wife Joan Monroe in the Diocese of Ross, a student at the Scots College in Rome, 1698. [RSC.I.124]

ROSS, GEORGE, a student at the Scots College in Rome, 1700. [RSC.I.125]

ROSS, Captain GEORGE, of the Royal Engineers, was killed on 9 December 1811 at the Siege of Ciudad Rodrigo, Spain. [SM.74.157]

SCOTS IN SOUTHERN EUROPE, 1600-1900

ROSS, HUGH, from Ross, a student at the Scots College in Rome, 1610. [RSC.I.103]

ROSS, HUGH, born 1627 in the parish of Coul, Aberdeenshire, son of Alexander Ross and his wife Mary Bonner, at the University of Aberdeen, a student at the Scots College in Madrid, Spain, 1647. [RSC.I.196]

ROSS, JAMES, born 1672, son of Thomas Ross and his wife Christine Dunbar in the Diocese of Ross, a student at the Scots College in Rome, 1697. [RSC.I.123]

ROSS, JOHN, Lieutenant Colonel of the Coldstream Guards, son of the late Admiral Sir John Lockhart Ross, and brother to General Sir Charles Ross of Balnagowan baronet, died on 28 July 1809 at the Battle of Talavera de a Reyna. [SM.71.717]

ROSS, JOHN, a volunteer under Garibaldi, 1860. [SHR.57.177]

ROSS, LAURENCE CLUNIES, born 1878, late of 26 Dundas Street, Edinburgh, fourth son of George Clunies Ross of the Keeling-Cocos Islands, died in Hotel Santa Catalina, Las Palmas, Grand Canary, on 2 February 1898. [S.17040]

ROSS, MARGARET ANKERVILLE, eldest daughter of the late General Ross, and grand-daughter of Lord Ankervill a Lord of Session in Scotland, married T. Akers Shone of the Royal Artillery, in Malta 1 March 1826. [SM.97.766]

ROSS, MARJORY, born 11 October 1782, in Logie Easter, daughter of Reverend John Ross and his wife Margaret Smith, died in Gibraltar during 1813. [F..7.69]

ROSS, THOMAS COCKBURN, Captain of the Portuguese Light Infantry, and a Lieutenant of the Queen's Regiment, eldest son of John Cockburn Ross of Shandwick, Ross-shire, fought at

SCOTS IN SOUTHERN EUROPE, 1600-1900

the Battles of Vimiera, Talavera, the Duora, and other combats in the Peninsula, died in London on 24 May 1813. [SM.75.479]

ROSS, ..., son of Lieutenant Colonel Robert Ross of the 20th Regiment, was born in Malta on 22 September 1804. [SM.66.972]

ROSS, ..., son of Colonel Archibald Ross, was born in Lisbon on 5 May 1818. [SM.82.101]

ROSS, ..., daughter of Lieutenant Colonel Ross of the 57th Regiment, was born in Gibraltar on 12 May 1808. [SM.70.717]

ROXBURGH, ARCHIBALD, born 1823, from Glasgow, died 20 March 1870, buried in the British Cemetery in Funchal, Madeira. [ARM]

RUFFIN, LOUIS, born in Turin, settled in Edinburgh in 1782 as a tambour manufacturer. [ECA.SL115.1.1]

RUSSELL, DAVID, from Fife, a student at the Scots College in Rome, 1613. [RSC.I.104]

RUTHERFORD, DAVID, from Fife, a student at the Scots College in Rome, 1610. [RSC.I.103]

RUTHERFORD, JAMES, a merchant in Madeira in 1814. [ARM]

RUTHERFORD, WILLIAM, a volunteer under Garibaldi in Italy, 1860. [SHR.57.175]

SANDEMAN, or FRASER, Margaret Chisholm, died in Rome on 14 March 1839, inventory, 1839, Comm. Edinburgh. [NRS]

SANDERSON, WILLIAM, a merchant in Malta, 1815. [NRS.CS41/13; CS42/13/110]

SCOTS IN SOUTHERN EUROPE, 1600-1900

SANDY, GILBERT, eldest son of the late George Sandy a writer in Edinburgh, died in St Lucar, Spain, on 22 January 1788. [SM.50.101]

SCOTT, ARCHIBALD, a merchant in Edinburgh, died in Malta, 4 May 1862, inventory, 1863, Comm. Edinburgh. [NRS]

SCOTT, CHARLES ANDREW, of Bridgeheugh, born 1817, eldest son of William and Alice Scott of Woll in Roxburghshire, died in Rome on 7 April 1838. [Protestant Cemetery in Rome, gravestone]; inventory, 1839, Comm. Edinburgh. [NRS]

SCOTT, Major FRANCIS, second son of John Scott of Whitehaugh, Roxburghshire, died at San Sebastian, Spain, in 1813. [SM.75.799]

SCOTT, GEORGE, of Cumming, Recoaro, Italy, died 26 August 1844, inventory, 1844, Comm. Edinburgh. [NRS]

SCOTT, HENRIETTA, born 1786, from Glasgow, wife of Thomas Muir of Muirpark, died 8 December 1844, buried in the British Cemetery in Funchal, Madeira. [ARM]

SCOTT, ISABELLA, daughter of James Scott in Glasgow, died in Lisbon, Portugal, on 10 January 1844. [W.V.429]

SCOTT, JAMES, born 1840, formerly of the 1st Edinburgh Artisans, a volunteer under Garibaldi, in Italy in 1860. [SHR.57.175]

SCOTT, JOHN, alias THOMAS FORBES, a student at the Scots College in Rome, 1649. [RSC.I.113]

SCOTS IN SOUTHERN EUROPE, 1600-1900

SCOTT, JOHN, from Duns, Berwickshire, settled in Madeira as a merchant around 1736, (ARM. Livros dos saidas # 252, fos. 53/69,
Arquivo Nacional da Torre do Tombo, Lisbon); a merchant in Funchal by 1754. [ARM]; died intestate in 1775 in York. [OW]

SCOTT, ROBERT, baptised in Duns, Berwickshire, 1708, to Madeira as a merchant during 1720s, moved to London around 1736. By 1739 he was a merchant in Madeira, possibly linked to the Scotts of Harden. [NRS.GD157.2267]; 1749, Robert Scott, merchant in Madeira and London, a deed of factory, [NRS.RD4.176/1.155]; he was trading with South Carolina in 1756. [NRS.GD219/290] [TNA.CO137.17] [CSPCol.XLIII, 1737] (Livros dos Saidas # 252, fos. 53/69, Arquivo Nacional da Torre do Tombo, Lisbon); probate 1 June 1771 PCC

SCOTT, ROBERT, a partner in the merchant firm of Newton, Gordon, and Murdoch in Madeira,1805. [ARM]

SCOTT, R., possibly from Glasgow, a volunteer under Garibaldi in Italy, 1860. [SHR.57.176]

SCOTT, THOMAS, from Reddleburn in Teviotdale, graduated MD from Glasgow University in 1732, a surgeon and physician in Porto, Portugal. [RGG]

SCOTT, THOMAS GRAY, Writer to the Signet, Edinburgh, born 1812, died in Madeira, 15 January 1856, inventory, 1856, Comm. Edinburgh. [NRS][Greyfriars gravestone, Edinburgh]

SCOTT, WALTER, baptised in from Duns, Berwickshire, 1706, emigrated to Madeira as a merchant during 1720s [TNA.CO137.17] [CSPCol.XLIII, 1737] (Livros dos saidas # 252, fos. 53/69, Arquivo Nacional da Torre do Tombo, Lisbon); .probate 2 July 1776 PCC

SCOTS IN SOUTHERN EUROPE, 1600-1900

SCOTT, WILLIAM, a Scots merchant and skipper, trading between London and San Miguel in the Canaries, 1587-1589. ['The Inquisition in the Canaries', RHS, London, 1912, p.73]

SCOTT, WILLIAM, a merchant in Madeira, married Jane Fleming, niece of James Fleming a merchant, in Madeira on 31 January 1792. [SM.53.152]

SCOTT, WILLIAM, late merchant in Madeira, son of the deceased Dr John Scott of Coats, died at Loanhead, 23 September 1809. [EA#XCII.4773]

SCOTT and Company, merchants at 72 Rua dos Ferrieros, Funchal, Madeira, 1811. [ARM][OW.137] [NRS.GD51.11.33.1-2]

SCOTT, PRINGLE, CHEAP, and Company, wine merchants in Madeira, 1766. [NRS.GD157.2267]; correspondence with America, around 1770. [NRS.NRAS.771, Bundle 377]

SCRIMGEOUR, or SKINNER, ALEXANDER, from Edinburgh, a student at the Scots College in Valladolid, 1636, and at the Scots College in Rome, 1641, later a Jesuit missionary in Scotland and England, died 3 September 1679. [RSC.I.112/195]

SCRIVENER, B., possibly from Glasgow, a volunteer under Garibaldi, in Italy, in 1860. [SHR.57.176]

SEATON, DAN, from Stirling, a volunteer under Garibaldi, in Italy in 1860. [SHR.57.177]

SEMPLE, GEORGE, brother of Hugh Semple, a student at the Scots College in Madrid, 1715. [RSC.I.200]

SEMPLE, HUGH, rector of the Scots College in Madrid, 1627-1654, [RSC.I.202]; in Madrid, 1635. [NRS.GD406.1.317]

SCOTS IN SOUTHERN EUROPE, 1600-1900

SEMPLE, HUGH, son of Robert Semple of Glasford and his wife Elizabeth Abercromby. a student at the Scots College in Madrid, 1715. [RSC.I.200]

SEMPLE, JAMES, a student at the Scots College in Valladolid, Spain, 1649. [RSC.I.198]

SEMPLE, JAMES, born 1645, son of the Baron Semple, a student at the Scots College in Valladolid, Spain, 1669, died in Madrid. [RSC.I.199]

SEMPLE, WILLIAM, son of John and Mary Semple, late of Glasgow University, a student at the Scots College in Madrid, Spain, 1647. [RSC.I.196]

SETON, ALEXANDER, from Aberdeen, a student at the Scots College in Rome, 1602. [RSC.I.101]

SETON, ANDREW, of Garleton, a student at the Scots College in Madrid, 1715. [RSC.I.200]

SETON, CHARLES, eldest son of Hugh Seton of Touch, died in Lisbon on 5 January 1773. [SM.35,54]

SETON, DAVID, from Fife, a student at the Scots College in Rome, 1612. [RSC.I.103]

SETON, GEORGE, from Aberdeen, a student at the Scots College in Rome, 1602. [RSC.I.101]

SETON, GEORGE, 5th Earl of Winton, a Jacobite in 1715, imprisoned in the Tower of London, escaped and fled to Rome, died there on 19 December 1749. [JCR.45][SM.10.54]

SCOTS IN SOUTHERN EUROPE, 1600-1900

SETON, JOHN, from Garleton, a student at the Scots College in Madrid, 1715, died in Edinburgh, 16 July 1757. [RSC.I.199]

SETON, PATRICK, from Fife, a student at the Scots College in Rome, 1602. [RSC.I.101]

SHAND, WILLIAM, born 1689, son of John Shand and his wife Margaret Shearer in Aberdeen, a student at the Scots College in Rome, 1712, died in Aberdeen, 27 September 1741. [RSC.I.128]

SHANKS, AGNES, born 1770 in Minorca, widow of William Hunter a sailor, died in Blackscroft, Dundee, buried 7 April 1844. [DCA.burial register]

SHANKS, JEAN, born 1774 in Minorca, died in Dundee, buried 6 February 1829. [DCA.burial register]

SHARP, JAMES, born 1768, son of Alexander Sharp in the Diocese of Aberdeen, a student at the Scots College in Rome 1782; died in Blairs College, Aberdeenshire, 14 April 1837. [RSC.I.145]

SHARP, JOHN, a student at the Scots College in Valladolid, Spain, 1785, a missionary as from 1796, died at Blairs, Aberdeenshire, 5 September 1860. [RSC.I.209]

SHARP, WILLIAM, a student at the Scots College in Rome, 1637, later a missionary in Scotland and England. [RSC.I.110]

SHARP, WILLIAM, a Colonel in Portuguese service, a birth brief, 1730. [LC#3115]; Sir William Sharp, baronet, born in St Andrews, Fife, a Major General in Portuguese Service, Governor of the province of Minho, Colonel of the Monca regiment of infantry, died in London on 13 February 1780. [SM.42.110]

SCOTS IN SOUTHERN EUROPE, 1600-1900

SHAW, MURDOCH, son of Roderick Shaw and his wife Fanetae MacNeil in the Diocese of the Isles, a student at the Scots College in Rome 1775. [RSC.I.143]

SHIELDS, JAMES, in Leghorn (Liverno), Italy, in 1845. [NRS.GD1.1123.7]

SHIRRESS, DAVID, eldest son of Reverend Dr Shirress in Aberdeen, died in Madeira on 15 December 1809. [SM.72.238][ARM]

SHIRRESS, JAMES, born 1793, son of Reverend D. Shirress of the University of Aberdeen, died in Madeira on 19 December 1813. [ARM][SM.76.237]

SIBBALD, WALTER, from Leith, died in Palermo, Italy, on 31 December 1814. [SM.77.237]

SILVER, GEORGE, of Netherley, born 1808, died in Funchal, Madeira, on 7 April 1843. [AJ#4973]

SIMONE, CHANELAIN, a merchant in Lisbon, Portugal, in 1715. [NRS.RD2.105.532]

SIMPSON, ALEXANDER, from Aberdeen, married Louisa Tully, daughter of Richard Tully late Consul in Tripoli, in Gibraltar on 19 March 1795. [SM.57.275]; in Gibraltar, later in Aberdeen, inventory 3 August 1807, Comm. Aberdeen. [NRS.CC1.W321]

SIMPSON, JAMES, the Russian Consul, married Harriet Mawby, daughter of Major Mawby of the 18th Foot, in Gibraltar on 2 December 1789. [SM.52.49]

SIMPSON, Colonel, born in Fife, of the Royal Imperial Marines, died in Trieste on 3 July 1820. [SM.86.287]

SCOTS IN SOUTHERN EUROPE, 1600-1900

SINCERF, JAMES, from the Diocese of St Andrews, a student at the Scots College in Rome, 1644. [RSC.I.113]

SINCLAIR, ALEXANDER, born in the parish of St Machar, Aberdeen, son of Walter Sinclair and his wife Mariota Douglas, a student at the Scots College in Madrid, Spain, 1647, later, a student at the Scots College in Rome, 1650, afterwards in Spain. [RSC.I.114/197]

SINCLAIR, FRANCIS, alias Don Francisco St Clair, Captain of Spanish Grenadiers, a prisoner at Berwick, 1747. [P.1.246]

SINCLAIR, GEORGE, a student at the Scots College in Madrid, 1710. [RSC.I.199]

SINCLAIR, JAMES, a student at the Scots College in Valladolid, Spain, 1776. [RSC.I.207]

ST CLAIR, Lieutenant Colonel JAMES, of the 87th Regiment of Foot, died in Madeira on 23 September 1807. [SM.70.398]

SINCLAIR, JAMES, possibly from Glasgow, a volunteer under Garibaldi, 1860. [SHR.57.176]

SINCLAIR, ROBERT, from the Diocese of St Andrews, a student at the Scots College in Rome, 1626, later a Jesuit in Italy. [RSC.I.108]

SINCLAIR, WILLIAM, a student at the Scots College in Rome, 1628. [RSC.I.109]

SKEEN or SKENE, Captain DAVID, from Dundee, died in Portugal, 1788. [Anglican Church Records, Lisbon]; inspector of military roads, died in Lisbon on 11 May 1788. [SM.50.258]

146

SCOTS IN SOUTHERN EUROPE, 1600-1900

SKENE, HELEN, daughter of George Skene of Rubislaw, died in Florence, Italy, on 20 July 1842. [AJ#4937][SG#1109][Florence gravestone]

SKENE, Mrs, wife of Captain Skene, eldest daughter of James Morison of Naughton, died in Lisbon, Portugal, on 19 January 1788. [SM.50.206]

SLADE, WILLIAM, of the Royal Navy, died in Florence, Italy, on 13 November 1825. [SM.97.384]

SLOAN, ALEXANDER, born 1754, son of William Sloan and Sara MacLoun, a student at the Scots College in Rome, 1772, died there. [RSC.I.142]

SLOANE, WILLIAM, son of Alexander Sloan, a student at the Scots College in Rome 1797. [RSC.I.146]

SMITH, ARCHIBALD, born 1794, from Glasgow, died in Madeira on 6 January 1823. [ARM]

SMITH, CHARLES, late Consul at Aleppo in Syria, died in Leghorn [Livorno], Italy, on 17January 1791. [SM.53.100]

SMITH, JAMES, from Moray, a student at the Scots College in Rome, 1671. [RSC.I.118]

SMITH, JOHN, from Aberdeen, a student at the Scots College in Rome, 1627, later a missionary in Scotland, [RSC.I.108]

SMITH, JOHN, from Dumfries, a student at the Scots College in Rome, 1639, later a Jesuit missionary in England and Flanders. [RSC.I.111]

SMITH, JOHN, born 1737, from Inverness, died in Gibraltar on 19 August 1812. [SM.74.805]

147

SCOTS IN SOUTHERN EUROPE, 1600-1900

SMITH, JOHN, eldest son of the late J. Smith a merchant in Inverness, died in Gibraltar on 28 October 1813. [SM.76.156]

SMITH, ROBERT, born 1765, master of the <u>Harmony of Aberdeen</u>, died in Zante on 21 August 1807. [SM.70.78]

SMITH, THOMAS, son of Robert Smith, a merchant late of Dunbeath, Caithness, died in Gibraltar on 20 March 1885. [S.13028]

SMITH, WILLIAM, a student at the Scots College in Valladolid, Spain, 1794. [RSC.I.211]

SMOLLETT, Dr TOBIAS, an author, died in the baths of Pisa, Italy, on 17 September 1771. [SM.33.558]

SNODGRASS, K., a Lieutenant Colonel in Portuguese Service, and a Major in the British Army, married Janet Wright, daughter of Peter Wright, in Paisley, Renfrewshire, on 30 May 1814. [SM.76.637]

SNODGRASS, MARGARET, second daughter of the late Reverend Dr John Snodgrass, Paisley, Renfrewshire, and sister of Lieutenant Colonel Snodgrass of the 1st Cacadores, married Benjamin Sullivan, Major of the British and Portuguese armies, in Lisbon on 15 January 1816. [SM.78.157]

SODORINI, Signior GASPARO, Ambassador of the Republic of Venice, was admitted as a burgess of Glasgow on 2 June 1787. [GBR]

SOMERVILLE, THOMAS, son of the Baron of Cambusnethan, Lanarkshire, a student at the Scots College in Rome, 1627. [RSC.I.108]

SCOTS IN SOUTHERN EUROPE, 1600-1900

SOMERVILLE, THOMAS, a student at Padua University, Italy, in 1633. [RCPE]

SOMERVILLE, WILLIAM, born in Minto, Roxburghshire, on 22 April 1771, died in Florence, Italy, on 25 June 1860. [Florence gravestone]

SOMERVILLE, ..., son of William Somerville, was born in Malta on 6 August 1807. [SM.70.77]

SOUES, EMMANUEL, born in Madeira on 2 February 1792, died at Lindores, Fife, on 22 April 1873. [Abdie, Fife, gravestone]

SPALDING, ALEXANDER, a student at the Scots College in Rome, 1633. [RSC.I.109]

SPIER, WILLIAM, son of Robert Spier of Burnbrae, Renfrewshire, died in Madeira on 20 March 1848. [SG#1711]

SPITTAL, Captain ROBERT, from Leith, died in Zea in the Mediterranean in 1817. [SM.79.585]

SPREUL, ROBERT or FRANCIS, a student at the Scots College in Rome, 1639, a Jesuit missionary, died in Scotland. [RSC.I.111]

SQUIRE, Lieutenant Colonel, of the Royal Engineers, eldest son of Dr Squire of Ely Place, Edinburgh, died in Truxillo, Spain, on 19 June 1812. [SM.74.646]

STABILINI, HERONYMI or GEROLAMO, born in Rome around1761, settled in Edinburgh 1784, 'for 23 years the Edinburgh Concerts', a resident of St James Square in 1794, died in Edinburgh during July 1815. [St Cuthbert's gravestone, Edinburgh] [SM.77.719][ECA.SL115.1.1][DM.1815.314]

SCOTS IN SOUTHERN EUROPE, 1600-1900

STARK, Mrs SARAH, wife of John Craig an architect in Glasgow, died in Barcelona, Spain, when bound for Italy, on 19 December 1792. [SM.55.50]

STEEL, WALTER, born 1799, from Peebles, died in Madeira on 21 November 1831. [ARM]

STENHOUSE, REBECCA, daughter of John Stenhouse a baker in Edinburgh, settled in Zante by 1841. [NRS.S/H]

STEUART, JAMES, Captain of the 3rd Battalion of the Royal Scots, second son of the late Andrew Steuart of Auchlunkart, Banffshire, was killed at San Sebastian, Spain, on 2 September 1813. [SM.75.799]

STEVENS, JAMES, born 1685, son of William Stevens and his wife Elisabeth Faulds in the Diocese of Glasgow, a student at the Scots College in Rome, 1703. [RSC.1.125]

STEVENSON, JOHN, born in Arbroath, Angus, during September 1815, died in Rome on 22 June 1879. [Protestant Cemetery in Rome, gravestone]

STEVENSON, JOHN, from Edinburgh, a volunteer under Garibaldi, in Italy in 1860. [SHR.57.177]

STEWART , CHARLES, Lieutenant Colonel of the 50th Regiment, aged 45, died in Corea, Spanish Estremadura, on 11 December 1812. [SM.75.158]

STEWART, DAVID, son of John Stewart of Dalguise, Perthshire, a merchant in Barcelona, Spain, a bond, 1768. [NRS.GD38.1.987]

STEWART, FRANCIS, born 1563, Earl of Bothwell, a rebel who fled from Scotland, died in Naples, Italy, in 1612. [SP.II.171]

SCOTS IN SOUTHERN EUROPE, 1600-1900

STEWART, Lady GEORGINA, daughter of the Earl of Galloway, died in Malta in 1804. [SM.66.479]

STEWART, H. M., in Cadiz, Spain, a commission with James Chalmers, 27 July 1792. [NRS.RD3.285.674]

STEWART, or TORIE, JAMES, a student at the Scots College at Valladolid, Spain, 1777, a schoolmaster in Aberdeen by 1825. [RSC.I.207]

STEWART, Colonel JOHN, of Invernity, Perthshire, a Jacobite in Urbino, Italy, in 1717. [JU]

STEWART, JOHN DRUMMIN, born in Newton, Inverness-shire, during 1822, from Logie, Banffshire, a Major General of the Bombay Army, died in Rome on 13 April 1874. [AJ#6589] [Protestant Cemetery in Rome, gravestone]

STEWART, PETER, sometime in Malta, later an inmate of Morningside Lunatic Asylum, Edinburgh, died in February 1859. [NRS.PS3.16/318]

STEWART, RICHARD, Major of the 43rd Light Infantry, died in Lisbon, Portugal, in October 1810. [SM.73.77]

STEWART, ROBERT, in Lisbon, Portugal, a letter, 1785. [PKA.ms101, bundle 80]

STEWART, ..., son of John Stewart the younger of Allanbank, was born in Naples, Italy, on 13 September 1779. [SM.41.510]

STICHEL, PATRICK, from Aberdeen, a student at the Scots College in Rome, 1602. [RSC.I.101]

SCOTS IN SOUTHERN EUROPE, 1600-1900

STINNEAR, NICHOLAS, born in Italy around 1805, a lamplighter in Edinburgh by 1851. [Census]

STIRLING JAMES, from the Canary Islands, was admitted to the Scots Charitable Society of Boston, 1716. [SCS]

STIRLING, JAMES, born 1827, son of Reverend James Stirling in Craigie, died 11 March 1846, buried in the British Cemetery in Funchal, Madeira. [ARM]

STIRLING, WILLIAM J., in Naples, a deed, 1886. [NRS.RD5.2082/262/223]

STODDARD, ..., daughter of Dr Stoddard H.M.Advocate in Malta, was born there on 26 May 1804. [SM.66.806]

STRACHAN, DAVID, in Malaga, a bond, 7 March 1773. [NRS.RD4.214.995]

STRACHAN, GEORGE, from the Mearns, a student at the Scots College in Rome, 1602. [RSC.I.101]

STRACHAN, JOHN, son of ......Strachan and his wife ...Hay of Dalgetty, Aberdeenshire, a student at the Scots College in Valladolid, Spain, 1664. [RSC.I.198]

STRACHAN, KENNETH FRANCIS, son of the Baron of Thornton, Rector of the Scots College in Madrid, 1717-1718. [RSC.I.203]

STRACHAN, ROBERT, from the Mearns, a student at the Scots College in Rome, 1612. [RSC.I.104]

STRACHAN, ROBERT, from Brechin, Angus, a student at the Scots College in Rome, 1634, later entered the Order of St Benedict in Germany. [RSC.I.110]

SCOTS IN SOUTHERN EUROPE, 1600-1900

STRACHAN, ROBERT, from the Mearns, a student at the Scots College in Rome, 1612. [RSC.I.104]

STRACHAN, ROBERT, born 1614, from the Diocese of Aberdeen, a student at the Scots College in Rome, 1679, died in Aberdeen on 28 March 1740. [RSC.I.120]

STRACHAN, THOMAS, from Aberdeen, a student at the Scots College in Rome, 1674. [RSC.I.119]

STRAUCHAN, WILLIAM, a Presbyterian minister in Gibraltar, 1840s, later in Constantinople. [F.7.556]

STRACHAN, WILLIAM, in Malaga, Spain, a deed of attorney with Robert Strachan, 10 May 1797. [NRS.RD2.283.500]

STRICKLAND, CHARLES, Major of the 82nd Regiment of Foot, died in Gibraltar, 1795. [SM.58.71]

STUART, CHARLES EDWARD LEWIS CASIMIR, born 31 December 1720, son of James Francis Stuart, Prince of Wales, son of King James, and his wife Princess Maria Clementina Sobieski, grand-daughter of King Jan Sobieski of Poland, died in Rome in February 1788. [SM.50.101]

STUART, CLEMENT, born in Batavia on 29 September 1746, son of Charles Stuart and his wife Elisabeth Jethon, a student at the Scots College in Rome, 1763. [RSC.I.139]

STUART, COSMO, born 30 April 1737 in the Diocese of Aberdeen, a student at the Scots College in Rome, 1752. [RSC.I.137]

STUART, DONALD, born June 1756, son of John Stuart and his wife Christine Grant in Elgin, Morayshire, a student at the Scots

College in Rome 1772, died in Elgin on 3 February 1820. [RSC.I.143]

STUART, JAMES EDWARD FRANCIS, the Chevalier de St George, born 10 June 1688, to France in December 1689, he married Princess Maria Clementina, daughter of James Louis Sobieski, Prince of Poland, in Boulogne on 28 May 1719, parents of Charles Edward Louis Stuart born 31 December 1720, and Henry Benoit Stuart born 6 March 1725 appointed Cardinal of York in 1747. James Stuart, after having resided in Rome for nearly 50 years, died there on January 1, 1765, and was buried in St Peter's. [SM.27.55]

STUART, MARGARET, daughter of Sir John Stuart of Allanbank, Berwickshire, married John Hippesley Coxe, in Rome in 1780. [SM.42.166]

STUART, Sir PATRICK, Governor of Malta, 1840s. [NRS.GD424.8.1/2]

STUART, PETER, formerly in Malta, died in Edinburgh, 23 February 1859, son of Peter Stuart, a merchant in Glasgow and Malta. [NRS.E870.11.2/3]

STUART, WILLIAM, from Dunblane, a student at the Scots College in Rome, 1617. [RSC.I.105]

STUART, WILLIAM, born 1668, from Glasgow, a student at the Scots College in Rome, 1688. [RSC.I.121]

STUART, ..., son of Colonel Patrick Stuart, was born in Corfu, Greece, on 6 October 1817. [SM.80.497]

STUART, Miss, niece of John Robertson of Ednam House, Berwickshire, married Ignace Malkousky, noble de Demavalden, Chevalier of the Order of St George, Major Commandant of the

SCOTS IN SOUTHERN EUROPE, 1600-1900

7th Imperial Battalion des Chasseurs at Santa Maria, Mola di Gaeta, and Commandant of the Imperial Chasseurs of the Two Sicilies, in Venice 16 April 1826. [SM.97.766]

SUTHERLAND, ANDREW, a Captain in the Royal Navy, and Commissioner of Gibraltar, died there in 1795. [SM.57.612]

SUTHERLAND, GEORGE, born 1839, from Edinburgh, died 11 December 1868, buried in the British Cemetery in Funchal, Madeira. [ARM]

SUTTIE, JOHN, a student at Padua University, 1666. [RCPE]

SYDSERF, JOHN, from Edinburgh, a student at Padua University, 1648. [RCPE]

TAIT, GEORGE, born in Spain around 1831, a mason's labourer in Edinburgh in 1851. [Census]

TAIT, JAMES HILL, born 31 August 1835, son of Reverend Adam Duncan Tait in Kirkliston, West Lothian, educated at Edinburgh University, ordained in Linlithgow 1861, a Church of England chaplain in France and Italy, died in Rome on 18 April 1900. [F.1.353]

TAIT, MATTHEW, aged 123, a tinker and a horner, died in Auchenleck, Ayrshire, on 19 February 1792. 'He served as a soldier at the Siege of Gibraltar in the year 1704'. [SM.53.153]

TAIT, ROBERT, Lieutenant in the Royal Navy, married Lucy Allen, daughter of John Allen a physician in Malta, there on 30 March 1819. [SM.84.94]

TAIT, ..., son of Robert Tait a Captain in the Royal Navy, was born in Malta on 2 August 1820. [SM.86.477]

SCOTS IN SOUTHERN EUROPE, 1600-1900

TARONE, ANTHONY, born in 1775 at Carrati, Lake Como, Duchy of Milan, Italy, a carver and guilder in Watson's Close, Murraygate, Dundee, buried in Dundee 4 December 1847. [DCA.burial register]

,

TARRES, JOHN, from Elgin, Morayshire, in Tangiers, 1678. [RPCS.X.546]

THOMPSON, Captain ALEXANDER, paymaster of the 53rd Regiment, died at Badajos, Spain, of fever on 21 September 1809. [SM.71.878]

THOMSON, DAVID, an engineer in Rome, a deed, 1874. [NRS.SC49.74.53]

THOMSON, JAMES, from the Diocese of St Andrews, a student at the Scots College in Rome, 1683. [RSC.I.120]

THOMSON, JAMES, son of Thomas Thomson and his wife Louis Shand in Aberdeen, a student at the Scots College in Madrid, 1734. [RSC.I.201]

THOMSON, JOHN, born 1742, son of William Thomson and Joanetta Barclay in the Diocese of Aberdeen, a student at the Scots College in Rome, 1759, died in Naples, Italy, in 1792. [RSC.I.139]

THOMSON, JOHN RAMSAY, died in Oporto, Portugal, on 7 January 1855. [St Cuthbert's MI, Edinburgh]

THOMSON, MARY GRAEME, born 1851, daughter of William Thomson of Balgowan, Perthshire, and his wife Margaret Cunninghame, died at Baths of Lucca, Italy, on 20 May 1910. [Protestant Cemetery in Rome, MI]

SCOTS IN SOUTHERN EUROPE, 1600-1900

THOMSON, WILLIAM, from Dundee, a student at the Scots College in Rome, in 1602. [RSC.I.101]

TODD, ANDREW, Captain of the 38th Regiment, was killed at the Siege of Burgos, Spain, on 31 October 1812. [SM.75.78]

TORRIE, CHARLES, assistant surgeon of the Brunswick Hussars, died in Corfu, Greece, on 11 January 1816. [SM.78.398]

TOUCH, THOMAS, from Aberdeen, a student at the Scots College in Rome, 1602. [RSC.I.101]

TRAILL, WILLIAM, of Woodwick, Orkney, married Miss Sarle, daughter of Charles Sarle of Lisbon, Portugal, there on 9 June 1817. [SM.79.583]

TRAQUAIR, Countess of, died in Madrid, Spain, 11 July 1796. [SM.58.577]

TRIGUETTI, MICHAEL, an officer in the service of the King of Sardinia and his charge d'affaires in Holland, was admitted as a burgess of Glasgow on 3 October 1786. [GBR]

TROTTER, THOMAS, a Lieutenant of the Royal Artillery, son of William Trotter in Edinburgh, died at Idanho Novo, Portugal, on 30 December 1812. [SM.75.238]

TROUP, HELEN GRAY, died 16 February 1896, buried in the British Cemetery in Funchal, Madeira. [ARM]

TUCKER, ..., an Ensign, a volunteer under Garibaldi, in Italy in 1860, was killed at Capua, Italy. [SHR.57.177]

TULLIS, WILLIAM, in Spain, letters, 1865. [NRAS.3223.TF5]

SCOTS IN SOUTHERN EUROPE, 1600-1900

TULLOCH, JOHN, a Lieutenant in the Royal Navy, died in Passage, Spain, in July 1808. [SM.70.639]

TULLOCH, Miss MARGARET HELEN, born 1795, daughter of Thomas Tulloch of Elliston, Roxburghshire, died in Rome on 20 February 1874, an inventory, 1874. [NRS.SC70.167.881] [Protestant Cemetery in Rome, MI]

TULLOH, Miss JANE, died at Castella Mare, Naples, Italy, in 8 October 1850, inventory, 1852, Comm. Edinburgh. [NRS]

TURNBULL, ISABELLA ARMOUR, born 25 April 1849, eldest daughter of the late John Turnbull of Glasgow and of Blairmore, Argyll, died in Rome on 9 December 1907. [Protestant Cemetery in Rome, MI]

TURNBULL, JOSEPH, from Cordale, died in Lisbon, Portugal, on 31 May 1802. [SM.64.616]

TURNBULL, THOMAS, born 1824, a farmer from Caithness, died 25 April 1849, buried in the British Cemetery, Funchal, Madeira. [ARM]

TURNER, JOHN, Lieutenant Colonel of the 75th Regiment, died in Palermo, Sicily, on 5 June 1813. [SM.75.718]

TWEEDALE, ..., a volunteer under Garibaldi, 1860. [SHR.57.175]

TYRIE, ADAM, at the Scots College in Valladolid, Spain, in 1775, later in Portugal. [RSC.I.205]

TYRIE, DAVID, from Brechin, Angus, a student at the Scots College in Rome, 1618, later a Franciscan monk. [RSC.I.106]

SCOTS IN SOUTHERN EUROPE, 1600-1900

TYREE, JAMES, from the Diocese of Brechin, a student at the Scots College in Rome, 1659. [RSC.I.116]

TYREE, JAMES, born in November 1700, son of David Tyree of Dennedir and his wife Anna Menzies in Aberdeen, a student at the Scots College in Rome, in 1717. [RSC.I.129]

TYREE, JOHN, born in 1696, son of David Tyree of Dennedir and his wife Anna Menzies in Aberdeen, a student at the Scots College in Rome, 1711, died in Shenval, 19 May 1755. [RSC.I.127]

UDNY, JOHN, son of James Udny from Aberdeenshire, British consul in Venice from 1760 to 1773, then in Leghorn [Livorno] Italy, from 1773 to 1800. [NRS.CS244/1483; GD2.420]; John Udney, British Consul General in Leghorn, married Selina Cleveland, in Leghorn, 21 August 1777. [SM.39.508]

URQUHART, JAMES, in Barcelona and Minorca, letters, 1712. [NRS.GD220.5.281]

VALENS, ROBERT, from Edinburgh, a student at the Scots College in Rome, 1610. [RSC.I.103]

VAN CORTLANDT, CATHERINE, wife of Dr William Gourlay of Kincraig, a physician in Madeira, died there on 9 July 1819. [SM.84.294]

VAN DUFFLE, JUAN, a merchant in Bilbao, Spain, trading with Inverness, 1714. [NRS.GD23.6.26]

VANS- AGNEW, CATHERINE, youngest daughter of the late Colonel Vans Agnew of Barnbaroch and Sheuchan in Scotland, died in Rome on 31 January 1872. [Protestant Cemetery in Rome, MI]

SCOTS IN SOUTHERN EUROPE, 1600-1900

VEITCH, HENRY, British agent and Consul in Madeira, 1810. [NRS.GD477.411]; married Margaret Antoinette Harrison, daughter of Thomas Harrison the Attorney General of Jamaica in 1808. [GM.78.1187]

VILLETTE, ALEXANDER, late Ambassador at the Court of Turin, Italy, was admitted as a burgess and guilds-brother of Edinburgh, 1769. [EBR]

WADDELL, ELIZABETH, born in June 1849, daughter of James Waddell of Stonefield, Glasgow, and his wife Rachel Anderson, died 27 September 1849, buried in the British Cemetery in Funchal, Madeira. [ARM]

WADDELL, JAMES, born 1825, from Stonefield, Glasgow, died 2 January 1850, buried in the British Cemetery in Funchal, Madeira. [ARM]

WALKER, JAMES PENMAN, a Lieutenant of the 20th Regiment of Foot, second son of Robert Walker of Wooden, died in Vittoria, Spain, on 19 October 1813 from wounds received in battle in the Pyrenees on 25 July 1813. [SM.75.960]

WALKER, JAMES, son of John Walker, died in Lisbon, Portugal, on 4 December 1841. [St Andrews, Fife, MI]

WALKER, JEAN R., Stafford Street, Edinburgh, and Italy, a deed of factory and commission, 22 May 1854. [NRS.SC20.34.30/193]

WALKER or ROSS, JOHN, a student at the Scots College in Rome, 1643, later a missionary in Scotland, died in Rome 1679. [RSC.I.112]

WALKER, JOHN, a surgeon in the service of the East India Company, died in Madeira in 1795. [SM.57.682]

SCOTS IN SOUTHERN EUROPE, 1600-1900

WALKER, LESLIE, escaped from French occupied Madrid, 1809, a letter. [NRS.GD26.9.536]

WALKER, MAGGIE, born 1880, daughter of Daniel Walker and his wife Jane Stone, died in Madeira and was buried in the British cemetery in Funchal on 22 July 1910. [ARM[

WALKER, ROBERT, from Aberdeenshire, a volunteer under Garibaldi, 1860. [SHR.57.177]

WALKER, ROBERT, a Baptist minister in Naples, son and heir to David Walker a merchant in Crossmichael who died 9 January 1889. [NRS.S/H.15.10.1891]

WALLACE, ALEXANDER, youngest son of the late Alexander Wallace a banker in Edinburgh, died in Madeira on 12 January 1810. [SM.72.317][ARM]

WALLACE, Mrs ANNE COLQUHOUN, relict of Lieutenant Colonel Goodwin Colquhitt of the 1st Foot Guards, died in Leghorn on 28 May 1828, inventory, 1841, Comm. Edinburgh. [NRS]

WALLACE, JOHN BAPTISTA, son of Franciscus Wallace a merchant in Lisbon, Portugal, was admitted as a burgess and guildsbrother of Ayr in 1664. [ABR]

WALLACE, WILLIAM, born 1773, a student at the Scots College in Valladolid, Spain, 1794, died 24 October 1854. [RSC.I.211]

WARDROP, ANDREW, a merchant in Madeira, married Christian Lundie, daughter of Archibald Lundie a Writer to the Signet, in Madeira on 26 November 1804. [SM.67.72]; Andrew Wardrop, born 1766, a merchant, died in Madeira on 22 March

SCOTS IN SOUTHERN EUROPE, 1600-1900

1833. [ARM]; Andrew Wardrop at Quinta Cova and Quinta da Levada, Madeira. [OW.36]

WARDROP, CHRISTIAN, daughter of Andrew Wardrop, died on Madeira 2 November 1813. [ARM]

WARDROP, JEAN, daughter of Andrew Wardrope a merchant in Madeira, was born there on 28 February 1806, [SM.67.318]; and baptised in the Anglican Church in Madeira on 9 March 1806

WARDROP, JAMES, son of Andrew Wardrop and his wife Christian Lundie, was born 15 February 1809 and baptised in the Anglican Church in Madeira on 7 March 1809. [ARM]

WARDROP, JAMES, in Madeira, a letter, 1827. [NRS.21.388]

WATERSTON, WILLIAM, in Minas de Rio Tulo, Huelva province, Spain, a sasine, 8 December 1913. [NRS.RS.Forfar.79/89]

WATSON, CHARLES, born 1791, died on Madeira, 13 August 1810. [ARM]

WATSON, ELISABETH, daughter of Alexander Watson , formerly of Billiter Square, married Nathaniel Green, HM Consul in Nice, in the British minister's chapel in Turin, Italy, in 1788. [SM.50.621]

WATSON, GEORGE, eldest son of William Watson of Auchtertyre, died in Athens on 15 August 1810. [SM.72.958]

WATSON, JAMES, son of Robert Lowson Watson and his wife Jane Hane Souter in Dundee, died in Madeira 17 March 1913. [ARM]

SCOTS IN SOUTHERN EUROPE, 1600-1900

WATSON, JOHN, British Consul in Venice, Italy, before 1798. [NRS.GD51.9.155]

WATSON, ROBERT, from Aberdeen, a student at the Scots College in Rome, 1646, died 31 July 1652. [RSC.I.113]

WATSON, ROBERT, from Moray, a student at the Scots College in Rome, 1666. [RSC.I.117]

WATSON, ROBERT, a cook, a Jacobite in Urbino, Italy in 1717. [JU]

WATT, WILLIAM COUBOROUGH, deputy inspector of the Naval Hospital in Malta, died in August 1848. [NRS.P3.16/225]

WATTERS, SUSAN, born in Spain around 1842, residing in Edinburgh by 1851. [Census]

WAUCHOPE, JOHN, of Niddry-Wauchope, a General of Spanish Infantry, was killed in Catelonia in 1718.

WAUCHOPE, Lieutenant Colonel, of the 20th Regiment of Foot, eldest son of Andrew Wauchope of Niddrie, died at Passages of wounds received on 2 August 1813. [SM.76.78]

WEBSTER, JEAN, wife of Thomas Webster the Customs Controller in Dundee, died 31 December 1818 on Madeira. [ARM][IJ.19.2.1819]

WEDDERBURN, ALEXANDER, a student at the Scots College in Rome, 1626, later a Jesuit. [RSC.I.108]

WEDDERBURN, JOHN, from Dundee, a student at the Scots College in Rome, 1602. [RSC.I.101]

SCOTS IN SOUTHERN EUROPE, 1600-1900

WEIR, JANET SPOTISWOODE, born in Edinburgh on 22 January 1824, died in Rome on 17 February 1883. [Protestant Cemetery in Rome, gravestone]

WEMYSS, CHARLES, a Captain of the 7th Fusiliers, died of wounds received in battle in the Pyrenees, 1813. [SM.75.720]

WEMYSS, FRANCIS HAMILTON, master of HMS Glatton, seventh son of the late William Wemyss a Writer to the Signet, died in Malta in May 1807. [SM.69.638]

WEST, JOHN, formerly a commissioner for the Customs in Scotland, died in Messina, Sicily, on 2 March 1770. [SM.32.167]

WHITE, EDWARD, a student at the Scots College in Rome, 1650. [RSC.I.114]

WHITE, Mrs JANETA CONTI, wife of Conte Cosimo Conti Aulii, counsellor to the Empress Queen, and Consul to their Imperial Majesties and to the Grand Duke of Tuscany at Genoa, daughter and only child of the deceased Robert White, HM Plenipotentiary in 1751 to the Kingdom of Tripoli in Barbary, descended from White of Bennachie, genealogy, 23 December 1769. [NRS.Lyon Office.GI.135]

WHITE, ROBERT, a merchant in Madeira, an inventory, 1875. [NRS.SC70.175.16]

WHITE, ..., British consul in Tripoli, died there in 1763. [SM.26.166]

WHITE, Lieutenant Colonel, died at Elvas on 8 June 1811 from wounds received when leading the 29th Regiment into action at the Battle of Albuera, Spain. [SM.73.637]

SCOTS IN SOUTHERN EUROPE, 1600-1900

WHITE, Mrs, wife of William Ramsay White, late surgeon in Leith now of the 27th Regiment, died in Sicily in 1811. [SM.73.640]

WHYTE, MELVILL, youngest son of the late Dr Whyte a physician in Edinburgh, died in Belle-Ritiro on 4 July 1779. [SM.41.399]

WHYTT, ROBERT, of Bennochie, an advocate, died in Naples, Italy, on 22 March 1776. [SM.38.221]

WIGAND, JOHN, possibly from Glasgow, a volunteer under Garibaldi, in Italy in 1860. [SHR.57.176]

WILLIAMS, JOHN, a mining surveyor, died in Italy before 1798. [NRS.GD51.9.155]

WILLIAMSON, Dr JOHN, Fellow of the Royal Society, Chaplain to the British factory in Lisbon, Portugal, died there 25 February 1763. [SM.25.301]

WILLIAMSON, WILLIAM, born 1841, late of the Royal Navy, a volunteer under Garibaldi, in Italy in 1860. [SHR.57.175]

WILLIMENT, ..., a factor in Spain, 1691. [NRS.AC7.9]

WILSON, ALEXANDER, late of Gibraltar, died in Kelso, Roxburghshire, on 1 December 1815. [SM.77.77]

WILSON, GEORGE FORTUNE, born 1875, a ships mate from St Andrews, drowned at Fiumicino, Italy, on 28 November 1922. [Protestant Cemetery in Rome, gravestone]

WILSON, JAMES, a Major of the Royal Regiment of Artillery, died in Gibraltar on 30 October 1794. [SM.56.801]

SCOTS IN SOUTHERN EUROPE, 1600-1900

WILSON, JAMES, MD, a British army doctor in Corsica, 1795. [NRS.NRAS.20.3]

WILSON, Captain JOHN, born 1887, from St Andrews, Fife, drowned at Fiumicino, Italy, on 28 November 1922. [Protestant Cemetery in Rome, gravestone]

WILSON, PETER, a printer from Ayr, died in Gibraktar on 3 May 1810. [SM.72.559]

WILSON, Lieutenant Colonel W. I., son of Robert Sym Wilson of Woodburn, Dalkeith, Midlothian, died in Varello, Italy, on 1 July 1893. [DC#12486]

WILSON, WILLIAM, a student at the Scots College in Rome, 1626. [RSC.I.108]

WILSON, WILLIAM, from Edinburgh, a volunteer under Garibaldi, in Italy in 1860. [SHR.57.177]

WINGATE, LOUISA JANE, born 1822, from Glasgow, youngest daughter of Andrew Wingate, died in Madeira on 16 April 1844, buried in the British Cemetery, Funchal, Madeira. [ARM] [W.V.464]

WINGATE, Captain, of the 74TH Regiment, aged 22, died at Salamanca, Spain, on 20 October 1812. [SM.75.78]

WINSTER, or DUNBAR, ALEXANDER, from the Diocese of Moray, a student at the Scots College in Rome, 1651, later a Jesuit missionary in Scotland. [RSC.I.114]

WINTON, the Earl of, a Jacobite in Urbino, Italy, in 1717. [JU]

WOOD, GEORGE, a student at the Scots College in Madrid, Spain, in 1693. [RSC.I.199]

SCOTS IN SOUTHERN EUROPE, 1600-1900

WOOD, JAMES, a Lieutenant of the 13th Regiment of Foot, died in Gibraltar on 19 April 1804. [SM.66.479]

WOOD, JAMES JULIUS, chaplain to the Black Watch in Malta, 1841-1843. [F.7.556]

WOOD, JOHN, commissary to the forces in the Mediterranean, died in Messina, Sicily, Italy, in 1809. [SM.71.558]

WOOD, JOHN, Captain of the 4th [King's Own] Infantry, and late Brigade Major to the Earl of Dalhousie, died in Portugal when serving under Lord Wellington, on 10 January 1811. [SM.73.153]

WOOD, PETER, born in Leith on 23 April 1802, third son of the late Christopher Wood, died in Rome on 6 February 1855. [Protestant Cemetery in Rome, MI]; of Frederick Street, Edinburgh, died in Rome, 6 February, 1855, inventory, 1855, Comm. Edinburgh. [NRS]

WOOD, SARAH, born 1826, daughter of Robert Wood, died 28 July 1845, buried in the British Cemetery, Funchal, Madeira. [ARM]

WYLLIE, GEORGE, acting Commissary General of a brigade under the command of the Marquis of Wellington, son of Robert Wyllie a manufacturer in Kilmarnock, died at Ciudad Rodrigo, Spain, on 19 November 1812. [SM.75.158]

YOUNG, ALEXANDER, from St Andrews, Fife, a student at the Scots College in Rome, 1626. [RSC.I.108]

YOUNG, JOHN, proprietor and publisher of the _Inverness Journal,_ died in Lisbon, Portugal, on 11 January 1815. [SM.77.238] [DM.1815.180]

SCOTS IN SOUTHERN EUROPE, 1600-1900

YOUNG, JOHN, of Glasgow, married Elisa Orsini, youngest daughter of Dr Alexander Orsini, Procurator at the Tuscan Law Courts, in Leghorn [Livorno], Italy, on 13 September 1854. [W.XV.1584]

YOUNG, ROBERT, born 1792 in Glasgow, died 8 July 1825 on Madeira. [ARM]

YOUNG, Captain, married Miss Fyers, eldest daughter of Lieutenant Colonel Fyers of the Engineers, in Gibraltar in 1802. [SM.64.615]

YOUNGSON, ANDREW, born in the parish of Durris, the Mearns, on 13 July 1619, son of Alexander Youngson and his wife Elizabeth Reid, educated at Aberdeen University and Marischal College, a student at the Scots College at Madrid, Spain, 1647, died 1679. [RSC.I.196/202]

YUILL, ARCHIBALD, master of The Loudoun of Glasgow, a galley, from Scotland to the Canaries or any port in Spain, in 1705. [CSPDom.iv.3223]

SOME SHIPPING LINKS

Adventure of Glasgow, a brigantine, master Thomas Fisher, from Port Glasgow to Madeira in August 1691. [NRS.E72.19.22]

Agnes and Jean of Ayr, from Ayr via Madeira and Barbados to Virginia, 1672. [TNA. CO33.16]

SCOTS IN SOUTHERN EUROPE, 1600-1900

Agreement of Glasgow, master Alexander Spinker, from Glasgow
bound for Cadiz, 1690. [NRS.E72.19.22]

Bachelor of Boston, from Port Glasgow to Madeira, 1691.
[NRS.E72.15.22]

Betty and Peggy of Montrose, master William Kenney, arrived
in Montrose on 13 October 1756 from St Uber in Portugal.
[NRS.E504.24.4]

Blandford, master James Lindsay, from Greenock to Madeira in
November 1761. [NRS.E504.15.10]

Crawford of Glasgow, master William Smith, from Greenock via
Gibraltar and the Canaries to South Carolina, 1752.
[NRS.E504.15.6]

Debsey of London, foreign built, 50 tons, master Thomas Glass,
22 man crew, from Dundee for the Canaries and the coast of
Barbary/Africa, January 1758. [NRS.S504.11.4]

Diligence, master James Addison, from Leith to Venice, April
1770. [NRS.E507.22.15]

Dolphin of Boston, from Glasgow to Madeira, 1686.
[NRS.E72.19.12]

Dolphin of Dundee, from the Canary Islands to Dundee, 1755.
[NRS.E504.11.3]

Eagle of Montrose, master Alexander Straton, from Montrose to
Venice in October 1756. [NRS.E504.24.4]

SCOTS IN SOUTHERN EUROPE, 1600-1900

Elizabeth of Glasgow, from Port Glasgow to the Canary Islands, 1690. [NRS.E72.19.22]

Elizabeth, master William Somervill, from Leith to Venice in July 1769. [NRS.E504.22.15]

Endeavour of Charlestown, New England, from Port Glasgow to Madeira,1689. [NRS E72.19.15]

Endeavour of Glasgow, master Peter Hawkins, from Port Glasgow bound for Fayal in the Western Islands, 1691. [NRS.E72.19.22]

Fair Susannah of Leith, master James Strachan, from Greenock to Madeira and South Carolina, 1751. [NRS.E504.15.5]

Fortune of Glasgow, master James Campbell, from Port Glasgow bound for the Canaries, 1690. [NRS.E72.19.22]

George of Leith, supercargo William Dunbar, from Leith to Lisbon, Cadiz and the Straits, 1679. [NRS.RH15.91.16]

George of Glasgow, master James McCunn, arrived in Port Glasgow from the Canaries, 8 April 1724. [NRS.CE60.2.264]

Good Intent of Perth, master William Bett, from Perth to Leghorn in 1765. [NRS.E504.27.5]

Gordon galley, master David Preshaw, from Leith to Leghorn in 1709. [NRS. Herring debs.]

Grandvale, master Robert Baine, and the Juno, master Thomas Ritchie, from the Clyde to Jamaica via Madeira, 1786. [G.Merc]

Helen of Inverness, master Alexander Stewart, from Inverness to Leghorn in 1726. [SIL#262]

170

SCOTS IN SOUTHERN EUROPE, 1600-1900

Henrietta, master John Smith, from Leith to Teneriffe in 1768. [NRS.E504.22.14]

Henrietta, master Robert Grant, from Leith to Teneriffe in 1769. [NRS.E504.22.14]

Hope of Bo'ness, master Matthew Robertson, from Cromarty to Bilbao, 1734. [NRS.AC9.1301]

Industry of Greenock, master William McCunn, from Greenock via Madeira to South Carolina, 1750. [NRS.E504.15.4]

James of Crawfordsdyke, master John Lorimer, from Glasgow to the Canaries in January 1695, arrived in March, sailed from Tenerife with a cargo of Madeira wine bound for Glasgow, captured by a St Malo privateer 18 April, cargo and most of crew taken prisoner, three crew on board with the privateers, anchored at Mount Bay, Cornwall, after privateers had abandoned ship, then the ship was looted and wrecked by local Cornish men. [GA.TD1619/82]

James and John of Greenock, master Hugh Wyllie, from Greenock via the Canary Islands to South Carolina, 1750. [NRS.E504.15.5]

Janet, from Glasgow to the Canary Islands, 1705. [Cal.SPDom.SP44.392.75]

Joan of Belfast, master Thomas Weir, from Port Glasgow bound for Madeira, 1690. [NRS.E72.19.22]

John and Marjory of Montrose, master John Sangster, arrived in Montrose on 20 October 1756 from Cadiz. [NRS.E504.24.4]

SCOTS IN SOUTHERN EUROPE, 1600-1900

Joseph and Daniel, from Ayr via Madeira to the Chesapeake, 1693. [NRS.B6.35.6, Ayr Archives]

Juno, master Thomas Ritchie, from the Clyde to Jamaica via Madeira, 1786. [G.Merc]

Katherine of Glasgow, from Port Glasgow to Madeira in October 1691. [NRS.E72.19.22]

Kinnoull, master Alexander Alexander, from Leith to Madeira in July 1769. [NRS.E504.22.15]

Kitty Graeme of Perth, master John Young, from Civita Vecchia to Perth in 1767. [NRS.E504.27.5]

Lark of Inverness, master George Roger, from Inverness to Leghorn in 1725. [SIL#237]

Lilly, from Glasgow via Teneriffe to Roanoke, North Carolina, 1768. [NCSA.PC67.21]

Loudoun of Glasgow, a galley, master Archibald Yuill, from Scotland to the Canaries or any port in Spain, 1705. [CSPDom.iv.3223]

Mally, master John La, from Leith to Gibraltar in July 1769. [NRS.E504.22.15]

Marigold of Belfast, master William Arbuckle, from Port Glasgow bound for Madeira, 1690. [NRS.E72.19.22]

Mary of Carron, master James Hamilton, from Dundee to Leghorn, Sept 1768. [NRS.E504.11.6]

Mary of Philadelphia, from Dunbar via Lisbon to Philadelphia, 1731. [NRS.AC9.1159]

SCOTS IN SOUTHERN EUROPE, 1600-1900

Mary Anne of Dundee, master Robert Birrell, from Dundee to Gibraltar, October 1758. [NRS.E504.11.4]

Middleton of Aberdeen, a galley, master Robert Middleton, from Inverness to Leghorn in 1721. [SIL#163]

Page, from Ayr to Madeira and Jamaica, 1751. [NRS.E504.4.2]

Peggie of Dundee, foreign built, 40 tons, master John Duncan, from Dundee to Gibraltar, July 1758. [NRS.E504.11.4]

Peggie, master Dougall Mathison, from Leith to Oporto, April 1770. [NRS.E504.22.15]

Phoenix of Dundee, from Madeira to Dundee, 1755. [NRS.E504.11.3]

Plain Dealing of Coleraine, master Samuel Wilson, from Port Glasgow bound for Madeira, 1690. [NRS.E72.19.22]

Providence of Irvine, master John Angus, from Ayr to the Canaries, 1690. [NRS.E72

Salisbury of Boston, from Port Glasgow to Madeira, 1689. [NRS. E72.19.15]

Stewart, master Alexander Auld, from Greenock to Madeira in January 1762. [NRS.E504.15.10]

't Huijs van Vreden, from Dundee to Genoa, Via Regia, and La Spetia, in 1604. [GAA.NA.99/29]

Venus of Perth, master John Nairn, from Perth to Venice in 1765. [NRS.E504.27.5]

173